SIGNALS THROUGH THE NOISE

Making sense of the digital economy —
through the people building it

Jamil Hasan

Copyright © 2026 by Jamil Hasan
All rights reserved.

No part of this book may be reproduced, distributed, or transmitted in any form or by any means, including photocopying, recording, or other electronic or mechanical methods, without the prior written permission of the author, except in the case of brief quotations embodied in critical reviews and certain other noncommercial uses permitted by copyright law.

This book is for informational and educational purposes only and does not constitute financial, investment, legal, or tax advice. The views expressed are those of the author and are based on personal experience, research, and interviews. Readers should conduct their own research and consult appropriate professionals before making financial decisions.

This work reflects the author's interpretations and perspectives. While based on interviews and real-world experiences, any conclusions or representations are solely those of the author. Reference to any individuals, companies, or projects does not imply endorsement or affiliation unless explicitly stated.

Digital asset markets are highly volatile and speculative. Past performance and discussed scenarios are not indicative of future results.

Some names, stories, and identifying details may have been modified to respect privacy.

First Edition · 2026
Published by Crypto Hipster Publications

ISBN: 978-1-972991-00-8

Cover design by Jamil Hasan
Interior design by Jamil Hasan

All trademarks and registered trademarks are the property of their respective owners.

Printed in the United States of America

For my sons, Chase and Jonathan —
who never stopped believing in me.

Signals Through the Noise

What if the noise isn't the problem—but what you choose to hear?

We are surrounded by information.

Endless opinions.
Endless predictions.
Endless urgency.

Markets move. Narratives shift. Timelines compress.

And somewhere in all of it, something real is happening.

But it doesn't announce itself. It doesn't trend. It doesn't demand your attention.

It builds quietly.

I didn't set out to write a book about crypto. Or AI. Or markets. Or technology.

I set out to understand people.

Over the past several years, I've had over 580 conversations with founders, entrepreneurs, and independent builders—people operating at the edge of what comes next.

Some were early. Some were wrong. Some were ahead of their time.

But all of them were trying to build something real.

What I found wasn't a set of answers. It was a pattern. A way of thinking. A way of seeing.
A way of filtering signals from noise.

This book is not about predicting the future. It is about recognizing it—before it becomes obvious.

If you are looking for certainty, you won't find it here.

If you are looking for shortcuts, this is not that book.

But if you are trying to understand what actually matters—beneath the noise, beneath the narratives, beneath the constant distraction —

Then you're in the right place.

This is not about price.

This is about signals. Not noise.

Preface

I'm Jamil Hasan. People call me the Crypto Hipster. I gave myself that name. I own it. It started as a joke. A meme. Then it became a signal. Not rebellion for rebellion's sake. Rather, a way of seeing things.

Crypto moves fast. Sometimes, a topic I spent several podcast episodes fully understanding in the first week completely changed the next week.

There is a tremendous amount of noise in the market and not enough uncovering of the true signals. I aim to change that.

Discussion about the price of Bitcoin, meme-coin hype, 1000X speculation, and narrative repetition never truly interested me. I wanted to find out what genuinely matters instead.

So, I started the Crypto Hipster Podcast in February 2021. Not to chase headlines. Instead, to have actual conversations with people building this space.

Founders. Creators. Thinkers...people trying to reshape systems.

Crypto Hipster became more than a podcast. Nine seasons. Over 580 conversations. Hundreds of written works.

Then I hit an uncomfortable fact:

Curating discussions is not the same as creating ideas.

For years, I documented conversations. Published transcripts of all my podcasts. Built an archive. A colleague told me that if I wanted to be an influential leader, I would have to do more than simply host conversations. I would have to move the conversations forward.

That person was right.

This book, which is the first of sixty-seven Crypto Hipster Curtain Calls compilations spanning two-hundred eighty-one interviewees, is the first part of that shift.

This book differs significantly from my first 399 books. It is not a collection of transcripts. It's an interpretation. A reflection. A synthesis of conversations, ideas, and lived experiences. It's where my voice meets the voices of the people I've learned from.

Crypto is not just technology. It's about power. About identity. About freedom. And above all, about people.

My path into this space came not from comfort. For the past five years, I have fought an aggressive desmoid tumor. What kept my mind busy and away from despair grew into something bigger. It became a way to process the world and my place in it.

This book blends two things:

1) The conversations I've had with builders of the digital economy.
2) And the lessons I have lived myself.

Conversations with others. And personal memoirs interwoven with them.

You'll see both here. You'll see ideas about decentralization and finance. About infrastructure and governance.

You'll also see stories. Resilience, failure, faith, relationships, recovery.

None of this technology exists in isolation. It reflects who we are. Too often, crypto gets reduced to price charts. The authentic story runs deeper:

a.) Whether these systems actually change anything or just recreate the same structures with a new label.
b.) Whether innovation leads to freedom or just a different method of control.
c.) Whether we, as individuals, choose to take part on purpose or just go with the current.

This book is my attempt to slow that down. To take hundreds of conversations and extract what matters most.

To connect patterns.

To ask better questions.

To share what I've learned. Not as answers. But as a framework for thinking.

This is not just my story. It's an invitation...an invitation to think differently. To question more. To build with intention.

I hope that if you see yourself in these pages, this book will serve as an inspiration for you to write your own story with more clarity, purpose, and conviction.

Table of Contents

Chapter 1—Come Back Different

The travel company iExplore had a tagline. "Come back different."

In April 2004, at sunset, I stood on Phnom Bakheng Hill, which is the primary lookout over Angkor Wat in Cambodia. I had two years of sobriety under my belt, and the view from that grassy hill was unlike anything I'd seen before. In that moment, I felt something I couldn't ignore—a presence that was loving and everywhere.

God had shown up before. Little foxhole prayers that somehow got answered. The Serenity Prayer that held me steady whenever I was just about to crack. Friendships that carried me through church basements and sober circles.

But this felt different. This time God was standing with me.

I didn't know what the tagline "come back different" really meant yet as it applied to my life. I certainly didn't know how that moment would shape the next twenty-two years.

Three weeks earlier, I was on a hill tribe trek outside Northern Vietnam. It was tough from the start. I was thirty-three, my back already failing, wrapped in a brace. Every step was uneven. The others were Australian and British students who moved as if they belonged there. Experienced trekkers. Comfortable, where I felt lost.

Rain came in sideways sheets. Nearly monsoon. The hills turned to mud. They laughed through it. I watched my footing, afraid to slip, trying not to fall behind.

I didn't belong.

Somehow, I finished the trek; but I finished on horseback and felt as though my journey was empty or incomplete. That first night, I slept on a bamboo bed under a huge mosquito net to keep malaria away. By morning, my back had loosened just enough to move.

They were glad I had made it. But when I told them where I was headed next, their tone changed. They didn't just question the plan.

They wondered if I could do it at all.

I left northern Vietnam carrying more than a sore back. I wasn't on vacation. I wasn't on assignment either. Two months earlier, I had sold all my furniture, moved out of my apartment, and left a job that didn't match my desire to be more spiritual. Looking back, I was a young man trying to figure out what my life was supposed to become.

Their doubt stuck with me. The quiet skepticism that maybe I was pushing too far. Part of me believed them. Another part of me kept going.

I didn't have words for it then. Something was pulling me forward. Past my discomfort, through my fear, and up against that overwhelming feeling of not belonging. I just knew I couldn't turn back.

Three weeks later, on that hill at sunset in Angkor Wat, everything changed. I said nothing. I didn't drop to my knees. There was no booming voice, no fiery sign, and not a single glowing lightbulb that went off above my head. It was quiet. But it was undeniable.

Standing there, looking at the ancient stone towers, surrounded by a thousand people yet feeling alone, I felt a peace I hadn't known before.

Not in addiction.
Not in early sobriety.
Not in the life I'd been trying to build.

For the first time, I saw that maybe my life wasn't something I had to force. Maybe it was something I was being led through. I wasn't just traveling. I was searching.

I didn't have the words then. Wouldn't for years. But I was not alone.

Over the next two and a half months, I ran into three major challenges. Two I chose. One blindsided me.

The first came in June 2004. A fifteen-mile hike along the crumbling ruins of the Great Wall of China. This was not the shiny, restored part of the wall that tourists visit. The stones were uneven, broken, and shifting. Entire sections had collapsed into jagged paths that demanded focus.

By then I had rebuilt some strength by backpacking through Thailand, Malaysia, and Singapore. My hike atop the ruins was not a casual walk. Each stone felt like the life I led before sobriety—fractured, unstable, unfinished.

But I was moving across it now. Step by step. I wasn't just walking on the Wall. I was learning how to move through broken ground. How to keep going when the path isn't stable. How to fall, get back up, and keep my footing. How to take in beauty without losing track of the next step.

I didn't know it then, but years later, those lessons came back when I navigated something just as unpredictable in the early days of crypto.

The second challenge was bigger and longer. A thirty-mile trek through Tiger Leaping Gorge, one of the deepest gorges in the world. Famous for its thousand-step initial ascent, the trail narrowed fast and hugged the mountain. Steep drops led to a roaring river. One wrong step wasn't a stumble. It was something worse: certain death.

There was no room for distraction. No room for doubt. Just forward. The air grew thinner. Climbs dragged on. Descents tested my balance. My legs burned. My back tightened again. I stopped sometimes to steady myself.

This wasn't just physical anymore.

It was mental.

Fear gets loud in places like that. It tells you to turn back, to play it safe, to stay within your limits. But something had changed since Angkor Wat. I still felt fear. I just didn't listen in the same way.

Step by step, I kept moving. Somewhere on that trail, I realized I had misunderstood courage.

Courage is not the absence of fear. It's recognizing fear and moving forward anyway.

When I finished the trek, I wasn't the same. I didn't feel out of place. I felt tested. For the first time, I thought I could handle what was in front of me.

The third challenge came out of nowhere. After Tiger Leaping Gorge, I felt unstoppable. Strong. Capable. Invincible.

And quietly, my old ego came back. The one that had fed my addiction. At first, it felt fine. Even earned.

After what I pushed through, why not feel powerful?

I forgot one thing: Strength without humility is dangerous, especially for someone with a history of alcoholism.

A few weeks later, I arrived in Kathmandu. My mind was already thinking bigger.

If I could do all this, why not climb Mount Everest?

Reality was simpler. I had two days before flying home. So, I did a day hike through Shivapuri

National Park, where the Himalayas begin. The air felt like something between heaven and earth. I carried that growing sense of power the whole day.

And then it happened.

Not on a cliff.

Not on a steep trail.

Something small: an ice cube.

I ordered a mango lassi.

It came cold with local ice.

I knew better. I drank it anyway.

That summer, during monsoon season, thousands in Nepal were dying from severe diarrheal illness. I read the headlines in the local Nepalese newspaper that the previous day there had been even more deaths. I dismissed that news as something that was just happening to the locals.

A parasite was spreading through contaminated water. It was microscopic. It was invisible. And suddenly, it was in me!

What followed was not a trek. It was an exit. Out of Nepal. Through Thailand. Into Taiwan. Back to New York, through John F. Kennedy International Airport, and then to my parents' home in New Jersey.

My body was breaking down. Weak. Dehydrated. Barely holding together. The same person who felt invincible days earlier was fighting just to get home.

The illness didn't pass quickly. It stayed with me for nine months. A slow, relentless reminder of something I had forgotten:

You are never as in control as you think you are.

Falling doesn't always come from obvious danger. Sometimes it comes from something as small... ...as an ice cube.

That ice cube sent out a million ripples.

iExplore's phrase came true.

I came back different.

Not only was I different. Everything was. The dream of continuous travel ended. In its place, I took a corporate job at American International Group in early 2005, just as I recovered. The backpack got replaced by a railroad apartment in Hoboken, New Jersey. The friends from my church group who had supported me through early sobriety no longer knew who I was.

I had no established career waiting for me. No structure to return to. Just the understanding that whatever came next, I had to build from the ground up.

I had to rebuild everything.

From scratch.

Back then, it felt like a massive loss. Years later, I would see it another way. When I became a customer of a crypto exchange that collapsed, I didn't panic like others. I had lived through starting over.

When my body failed me again, dual heart attacks in 2018 and later a five-year ongoing battle with a desmoid tumor, I didn't face it as something new. I have been here before. I knew what it meant to lose everything.

More importantly, I knew how to come back.

This time I wasn't doing it alone. I had my family beside me. And something else I didn't fully get back then: A quiet, steady belief that even in setbacks and losses there was still a path forward.

Looking back, I can see it now. None of it was random. Not the struggle. Not the doubt. Not the times I felt out of place. Not even the fall. God doesn't hand you anything he thinks you cannot handle.

Each step, through broken ground, along narrow edges, into places I never expected, was shaping something I couldn't yet see.

I thought I was learning to survive; God was teaching me how to trust.

Trust that I didn't have to control everything.

Trust that when I lost my footing, I wouldn't be left there.

Trust that there was a path even when I couldn't see it.

I didn't understand it then. But I do now. The moment on that hill overlooking Angkor Wat wasn't the end.

It was the beginning of a life I would spend the next two decades trying to understand.

Chapter 2—I Belong Here—And So Do They

The first time I said, "I belong here," it felt like something I had to prove. Now I understand something different.

Belonging isn't about having already arrived. It's about recognizing that you're walking in the same direction as the people who have.

During my one-year apprenticeship at The Digital Economist, I found myself surrounded by people who, on paper, had done more. Built more. Scaled more. Achieved more.

Experts. Operators. Founders. People with outcomes that could be measured.

And for a moment, that old question surfaced again:

Do I really belong in this room?

But this time, I didn't stay committed to doubting myself. Because I saw something I hadn't fully understood before. We weren't connected by titles. We were connected by perspective.

By what we recognized was coming.
By how we thought about systems, incentives, and the future being built in real time.
By the willingness to step into something uncertain and shape it anyway.

They had results. I had experience. They had built companies. I had spent years listening to, learning from, and translating the thinking of builders across the digital economy.

Different paths. Same direction.

And that's when it clicked:

Belonging isn't granted at the finish line; it's recognized along the way.

Then I realized there comes a time when belonging stops being internal and becomes visible instead.

For me, that moment happened at the Consensus 2024 blockchain conference in Austin, Texas.

I was there hosting the Crypto Hipster podcast interviews in the media lounge. Not attending; rather, I was working. I was recording conversations with builders shaping the digital economy in real time. I titled those podcast episodes: "Crypto Hipster On the Ground."

And something unexpected happened. Out of all the interviewers in the room, I had the second-longest line. The only person with a longer line was Navroop Sahdev.

Navroop isn't just the founder and CEO of The Digital Economist (TDE). She's an economist and technology futurist operating at the intersection of blockchain, AI, and global economic systems. TDE is a platform and an ecosystem that convenes leaders, policymakers, and builders working to shape a more human-centered digital economy.

That wasn't the first time we had met. A few years earlier, I had moderated a roundtable at an online crypto conference where she was participating. At that time, she said something simple, which she said to me again at Consensus:

"Maybe someday we can collaborate."

It felt like a possibility the first time. Standing there in Austin, it felt like alignment.

Months later, I received an email from The Digital Economist announcing applications for their Senior Executive Fellowship. I didn't hesitate.

I recognized it.

This wasn't about trying to enter a new world. It was about stepping further into one I was already operating in.

I applied. And in September 2024, I began the fellowship.

Along the way, I collaborated closely with four individuals whom you're about to meet. Each of them accomplished. Each of them is building. And each of them reinforced something I understood more clearly than ever:

Belonging isn't about being the most accomplished person in the room. It's about knowing you're in the right room.

Some people build companies.

Others build frameworks for how the future should work.

Nikhil Varma sits at the intersection of both.

As the head of the blockchain working group at The Digital Economist, and a computer engineer with a career spanning entrepreneurship, academia, and emerging technology, his path reflects both depth and range. He founded and exited a company, pursued an MBA, and completed a PhD in operations management using artificial intelligence. Nikhil brings a system-level understanding to everything he touches.

On paper, he's accomplished.

But that's not what stood out to me. What stood out was how he thought.

Working alongside him during the fellowship, I quickly recognized Nikhil doesn't see blockchain as speculation or hype.

He sees it as infrastructure.

Nikhil sees blockchain as a tool to solve real-world problems—particularly in sustainability, where environmental, economic, and social forces must be balanced together.

He described it as a three-legged stool. Remove one leg, and the system fails.

That framing alone tells you something. It's not the language of someone chasing trends. It's the language of someone building systems meant to last.

His work with the Algorand Foundation reflects his philosophy of focusing on energy-efficient, carbon-negative infrastructure and exploring how transparent, verifiable systems can support sustainability initiatives across the globe.

From bio-digester projects in developing regions to digital monitoring systems that prevent greenwashing, Nikhil's focus is consistent:

Use technology to improve lives—at scale. And do it responsibly.

That's the signal.

Because belonging in this space isn't defined by noise. It's defined by intent...by whether someone is building something that matters.

Nikhil isn't just participating in the digital economy. He's helping shape how it develops, which is toward something more sustainable, more transparent, and more human.

That's why he belongs here. And that's why he's here.

Some people study systems. Others question whether the systems themselves are still serving us.

Dr. Shruti Shankar Gaur does both.

As a Senior Fellow and Program Director at The Digital Economist, her work spans the intersection of artificial intelligence, blockchain, and human development. Her background reflects that range. Shruti has a foundation in organic chemistry, a PhD in inclusive education, and leadership in building more equitable learning systems.

On paper, she's accomplished.

But what stood out to me wasn't just her credentials. It was her urgency.

Working alongside her during the fellowship, I learned Shruti doesn't see AI as a tool we simply adopt. She sees it as a force actively reshaping human civilization. Not gradually. But all at once.

She described it as a tidal shift: one that doesn't just change how we work, but how we think, learn, and define what it means to be human.

And that's where her focus lies: not just in innovation, but in responsibility. Without ethical guardrails, artificial intelligence can move faster than our values.

AI mirrors our consciousness, while blockchain reflects our desire for trust, transparency, and decentralization. Neither delivers those outcomes automatically.

They require intention. They require alignment. And most importantly—they require us to grow alongside them.

That's the signal.

Shruti isn't just taking part in conversations about the future. She's asking whether we're even asking the right questions.

That's why she belongs here.

Some people wait for the right moment to build, while others build because the moment demands it.

Jean Criss is firmly in the second category.

As the founder of Jean Criss Media and Crisscross Apparels, and a Senior Executive Fellow at The Digital Economist, her work sits at the intersection of technology, media, and entrepreneurship.

On paper, she's accomplished. But what stood out to me wasn't just what she's built. It was how she builds.

Working alongside her during the fellowship, I saw how Jean integrates technology (blockchain, AI, media) not as separate ideas, but as tools to solve actual problems.

Her journey into entrepreneurship began with disruption. After being laid off—and facing a breast cancer diagnosis—she built anyway. Within thirty days, she launched her business. It wasn't a perfect launch, but she created momentum.

From wearable technology supporting breast cancer recovery to blockchain-based data systems, her work reflects innovation grounded in purpose.

That's the signal.

Because belonging isn't about perfect conditions. It's about building through imperfect ones.

That's why she belongs here.

Some people build within systems. Others work to connect them. Tristan Thoma operates in the space between.

As Managing Director of Impera Strategy and a collaborator within The Digital Economist, his work focuses on integrating decentralized technologies into real-world systems.

On paper, he's accomplished.

But what stood out to me was his focus on implementation.

Working alongside him during the fellowship, Tristan sees blockchain not as an isolated revolution but as an integration challenge.
His work spans continents—from combating modern slavery to enabling financial inclusion on a global scale.

He understands that the future won't be built in isolation. It will be bridged.

That's the signal.

And that's why he belongs here.

Different paths. Different disciplines. Different expressions of what it means to build in a world that is still taking shape.

And yet, the common thread is unmistakable.

Nikhil builds systems designed to last.

Shruti questions whether those systems reflect the values we need.

Jean proves that ideas only matter when they're brought into the real world.

Tristan works to connect it all—across institutions, borders, and realities.

Individually, they are accomplished. Collectively, they represent something more.

A signal: not on where the digital economy is, but of where it's going.

And standing alongside them, what I came to understand is this:

Belonging isn't defined by how far you've already gone.

It's defined by whether you're moving in the same direction as the people helping shape what comes next.

That's the thread that connects all of us.

Different stages. Same alignment.

And once you see it clearly, the question changes.

It's no longer "Do I belong here?"

It becomes:

"What am I building now that proves it?"

Chapter 3—Driving Economic, Environmental, and Social Advancement

Dr. Nikhil Varma is an Associate Professor of Management at the Anisfield School of Business, Ramapo College of New Jersey, and a globally recognized expert in blockchain technology, operations, and sustainability. With over twenty years of academic and professional experience, he bridges the gap between research and practice in emerging technologies and management.

Dr. Varma serves as the Senior Fellow and Chair of the Blockchain Workgroup at The Digital Economist and is the Technical Lead for the Algorand Foundation in India, where he supports blockchain diffusion and adoption across the country. His work focuses on leveraging decentralized technologies to drive innovation and sustainable growth.

Holding a Ph.D. in Business Administration and an MBA from HEC Montréal, along with advanced engineering credentials, Dr. Varma has published extensively on supply chains, sustainability, and blockchain applications in top-tier journals and global conferences. He is also a sought-after advisor, having supported ventures like Aten Ventures and Qbrics.

At Ramapo College, he designs and teaches cutting-edge courses in Business Analytics, Data Visualization, and Sustainability, equipping students with real-world skills in data-driven decision-making. A certified Scrum Master and SAP professional, Dr. Varma combines technical expertise with strategic insight to advance the adoption of blockchain and emerging technologies globally.

Podcast Guest: Dr. Nikhil Varma
Podcast Date: February 4, 2025, Season 8

Podcast Link:
https://open.spotify.com/episode/7IDeOFCeOc8E
AaomFr5kSU?si=TRro7ce5QuW8SRRYwJ-eGA

****

Some people build things. Others step back and ask a different question.

"What system are we actually building?"

For a long time, I didn't think that way. My world was movement. Execution, conversations, momentum. Episode after episode. Book after book. Produce, produce, produce!

I measured progress in output. Episodes recorded. Conversations finished. Ideas saved. The more I produced, the more I felt like I was moving forward.

For a while, that was enough. It gave me direction, even if the direction was fuzzy. Over time, something felt incomplete. Not wrong. Not unethical or unjust. Just incomplete. Under all the conversations, under all the energy I spent to get the high of that next adrenaline hit, and after all the conversations about innovation, I noticed something I couldn't ignore:

> We weren't just building companies, blockchains, or technology anymore. We were building systems that other people would depend on.

That realization carries weight. When people depend on something, failure is more than a missed opportunity. It has consequences. It changes behavior, choices, and outcomes beyond the builder. I didn't understand that level of responsibility until I spoke with Nikhil Varma.

Nikhil doesn't play this game like most people. He isn't reacting to market cycles or chasing trends. He thinks in systems. Trained as a computer engineer, his past work was in mission-critical environments. In these environments, failure isn't theoretical. It's catastrophic.

That background colors how Nikhil looks at everything. "When failure has real consequences, your thinking shifts. You stop asking if something works in ideal cases. You ask what happens when it does not."

You care less about raw performance and more about whether that creation, innovation, or invention can survive stress.

That sounds small, but it changes the design. Most spectators (influencers, hobbyists, fans, enthusiasts) of crypto do not think that way. Their lenses are the speculative "upside," opportunity, and speed. Growth gets cheered. Adoption gets cheered. Momentum gets cheered. How much Bitcoin Michael Saylor's Strategy buys makes headlines. But the big questions are rarely asked:

What happens when this fails?

Who takes the hit?

Does the system survive stress or does it crumble?

Nikhil asks these tough questions: "The question isn't whether something works. It's what happens when it doesn't."

And those questions made me think. I looked at my approach and saw I'd been moving a lot, headed nowhere more quickly than others.

Stay active.

Be visible.

That makes forward motion, sure.

It doesn't make for stability.

Eventually, I had to admit something simple. Movement is not the same as direction. Output is not the same as substance.

Speed often hides fragility. Nikhil has seen this play out in markets. Assets that look strong while they're rising, although backed by attention, liquidity, and story, can fall apart when conditions change. When that happens, you see what was always there but hidden by motion. The structure wasn't built to hold. It was built to move.

That's the distinction Nikhil kept pointing to. His path shows that shift.

Like many in this space, he built early. Founded a company, sold it, and kept building. Then the market turned, and he rebuilt. That part is familiar. What he did next is not.

Instead of jumping into the next big thing, he dug in. He earned an MBA, worked in consulting, and finished a PhD in operations management using AI.

That sequence signals a different priority: no longer optimizing for speed, but optimizing for understanding.

That matters.

Speed can get you ahead. Understanding decides whether you can stay there. Without it, you're at the mercy of favorable conditions. With it, you can adapt.

When blockchain entered Nikhil's thinking, it wasn't fresh the way it was for others. His background in distributed systems meant he already saw decentralization as an architecture, not just a story. But he saw more in blockchain than simply infrastructure. "Blockchain isn't about money. It's about verification."

He saw a way to rethink how trust is coordinated across systems.

That's a different level of abstraction. It moves the focus from single products to the structure beneath them.

Most people in crypto are building products. Nikhil thinks about the systems that products rely on. That shift changes things. How you judge success changes. How you weigh risk changes. How you define progress changes.

When we talked about sustainability, he broke it down into three parts. One is the environment. Another is the economic side. The third is whether people are aligned socially.

"Sustainability only works when environment, economics, and social alignment all hold. Remove one, and the system breaks," Nikhil asserts.

The framework seems simple, so it's easy to miss, but the implications are wide. It applies to almost any system. A project that makes economic sense but is rejected by people won't scale. One that people accept but can't pay for will fail. One that meets both but lacks structural integrity will break under pressure.

Once you think this way, you spot patterns in failure. Some systems rely on endless capital inflows that aren't sustainable. Others can't handle volatility or scale. Some fail because people don't use them the way the designers expected.

These failure modes aren't hypothetical. They're visible. In crypto, I have seen fragile systems pull off huge short-term wins. A powerful story plus liquidity and attention gives the appearance of durability. But if you change the environment, the weak points show.

Price is not proof.

Momentum is not durability.

Attention is not a structural foundation.

What matters is whether the system underneath can take pressure. That's the lens Nikhil uses when stress-testing systems.

Most people evaluate things in calm conditions. They check performance when liquidity is high, sentiment is good, and participation is rising. In those moments, almost everything looks fine. Growth hides flaws. Momentum smooths over weak points.

But systems are not defined by how they act when everything works. They're defined by how they act when something breaks. Nikhil claims, "Most systems don't fail immediately. They fail under pressure."

Stress testing matters. A system that holds under pressure keeps working when inputs change. It doesn't rely on perfect conditions to survive. It adapts when variables shift. That sounds like something else to me, too: our human condition.

Instead of collapsing when assumptions fail, fragile systems behave differently. They need continued growth, participation, or belief. The moment one of those slips, the system unravels. That's the gap between resilience and conditional stability.

Look through that lens and your questions change. You stop asking how high something can go. You ask how much it can withstand.

Another shift Nikhil pushed was how to think about blockchain. To him, blockchain is not mainly about money; it's about verification. Most systems depend on trust, reporting, and delayed checks.

Information is collected, processed, and reviewed later. That adds delay and opens the door to manipulation. Blockchain lets data be recorded at the source and secured so it can't be altered.

Verification becomes embedded instead of external. That is foundational. But it also creates tension. Systems can develop fast. People do not. Technology can enable transparency. It can't make people ready for that transparency.

Over the years, I've met many people who detest blockchain but cannot explain why, or even what blockchain is. That disconnect between animosity and understanding has much to do with being ready for transparency. The gap between what a system can do and how people behave is where many implementations hit resistance.

We then talked about incentives, which sit at the center of how systems work. Systems don't change behavior directly. Incentives do. People respond to rewards and consequences.

Nikhil focuses on designing systems where the desired behavior aligns with incentives. Where doing the right thing is the easiest thing to do, as well. That alignment lets systems scale without constant policing. Without it, you need enforcement. With it, things run more naturally. Dr. Varma says, "If a system depends on perfect conditions, it's not a system—it's a scenario."

This perspective also changes how one reads crypto's noise. Speculation alone isn't the problem. Confusion is. When participants can't tell value from story, or progress from activity, systems wobble.

Nikhil has watched those cycles. So have I. Attention-driven cycles unwind fast. When they do, you see what was sustainable and what was not.

Looking ahead, the convergence of tech adds another layer. AI, the Internet of Things, and blockchain are growing side by side. AI helps decision-making. IoT captures real-world data. Blockchain handles verification. Together they let data be captured, interpreted, and secured.

And together, they raise a new challenge.

If content, decisions, and interactions can be generated artificially, verifying what's real becomes essential. That's where blockchain's role grows.

After speaking with Nikhil and working with him at The Digital Economist, I now notice things I missed before when I first started my podcast journey.

Before, I didn't question the structure underneath. But now I see patterns.

Movement versus direction.

Activity versus durability.

Things that look strong versus things that are strong.

Once you understand systems can fail even when they look strong, you act differently. You become more selective. More intentional. Focused on what holds despite market conditions and external realities like inflation, market panic, and war. After talking with Nikhil, I didn't leave excited in the usual way. I left clearer. The digital economy isn't only about making new things. It's about building systems that work in the real world.

The question isn't what to build next. The question is whether what we build will hold best.

That's the difference between momentum and permanence.

Chapter 4—How an AI Revolution Will Lead to Human Evolution

Dr. Shruti Shankar Gaur is a polymath and thought leader working at the intersection of education, inclusion, diversity, policy, and innovation. Holding a Ph.D. in Inclusive Education, she has been honored with a University Gold Medal and the Certificate of Academic Excellence by India's Ministry of Human Resource Development, reflecting her commitment to transformative change.

As founder of Research & Innovation in Education (RIEDU), she leads initiatives like the Young Editors Program, fostering young global writers focused on inclusion and diversity. Inspired by UN SDG 4.5 and 4.7, her work includes teacher training workshops, academic publishing, and her poetry collection, Four Decades.

At The Digital Economist, she served as Program Director at the Center of Excellence, managing the fellowship program and interdisciplinary collaborations. She has represented the organization at G20 India, the World Economic Forum in Davos, and Cannes Lions, contributing to global discussions on AI, policy, and socio-economic transformation.

Beyond policy, she is a Creative Partner, Mentor, and Strategist at Sankarsingh-Gonsalves Productions in Canada, advocating for culturally inclusive storytelling. In New Delhi, she is Director of Research, Innovation, and Inclusion at ae-research, leading the launch of its first DEI Lab.

Dr. Gaur's work spans education, policy, and creative industries, ensuring a lasting impact on global inclusion, equity, and innovation. Whether mentoring young writers, shaping policy, or driving research, she remains a catalyst for transformative change.

Podcast Guest: Dr. Shruti Shankar Gaur

Podcast Date: March 12, 2025, Season 8

Podcast Link:

https://open.spotify.com/episode/0pNebtxyVB4m

OGkSufSHt2?si=CRXwQVSJTyCiHXZRTTxdXA

****

There's a kind of discomfort that doesn't come from failure. It comes from progress.

Not when things break.

Rather, when they work. When they speed up and scale. And you're not sure they should.

I've felt that in the crypto industry watching markets surge and collapse, witnessing catastrophes and bankruptcies, and experiencing market winters and bear cycles. Though lately, it's AI that's gotten to me most.

For the first time, it doesn't feel like we're just building tools. It feels like we are actively reshaping how we think, how we relate, and who we are.

My conversation with Dr. Shruti Shankar Gaur was a memorable one. Not because she had answers. Because she asked questions most people avoid.

Shruti didn't come from a typical tech path. She started in organic chemistry, moved into education, and then focused on inclusive education at the doctoral level. She's spent years studying how people learn, how they relate, and how deep beliefs shape behavior. That way of looking at things changes everything.

When she looks at AI, she doesn't start with capability. She starts with consequences. She said, "We are scared of the unknown...and AI is venturing into the unknown."

That line cuts through the mess. It explains why this moment feels different. We've seen big tech shifts before. The internet and smartphones, and social platforms have changed how we live and connect. But none of them hit home like this. AI does.

Shruti then said something that I remember more than anything else. "AI is a mirror of human consciousness." I found that to be an uncomfortable idea. Because it means whatever we put into these systems will reflect who we are.

Not who we think we are. Who we actually are when our patterns are scaled and returned to us.

Then the talk moved beyond tech. If AI is a mirror, it doesn't just show capability. It shows bias, assumptions, limitations, and contradictions. It shows what we built into the system. And what we carry inside ourselves.

What makes this moment different isn't only what AI can do. It's what it represents underneath.

For most of human history, intelligence helped shape identity. It marked expertise. It decided who teaches and who leads.

AI disrupts that. When machines can generate language and simulate reasoning, the line between human intelligence and system intelligence blurs. That uncertainty creates discomfort.

If a system produces something that looks like insight, what counts as actual insight? If it creates content, what counts as original thought? If it responds intelligently, what counts as understanding?

These aren't engineering questions. They are identity questions. And they don't have instant answers. Which is why this moment feels different.

Previous tech mostly extended what humans could do. This one challenges what humans are.

I've worked in places that reward speed. Crypto moves fast. Narratives move faster. Now AI speeds everything up even more.

Talking with Shruti forced me to stop and ask a tougher question: Are we evolving on purpose or just reacting faster?

She drew a line between forced change and conscious change. Forced change happens because systems move, and we adapt to keep up. Conscious change requires awareness, intention, and reflection. Right now, most of this feels forced. And that is risky. When change outpaces understanding, we lose direction. We move forward, but without a clear sense of where we're headed or why.

There's another layer under the usual AI talk: substitution. Not only of tasks but of perceived value. AI doesn't just replace doing. It overlaps with thinking. That causes tension.

People get value not only from what they make; they get value from how they think and how they contribute ideas. When AI enters space, it threatens more than output. It threatens identity. That's a big part of the unease.

One thing that sank in for me in my conversation with Shruti was the gap between output and meaning. AI is great at output. It can generate text and synthesize information. But the output is not meaning.

Meaning comes from context, experience, memory, and interpretation. Humans don't just respond. We assign weight to responses. AI doesn't do that. It is produced from patterns. And because the patterns are coherent, it looks meaningful. But appearance is not understanding.

When people rely on output without wrestling with meaning, things shift. Depth drops. Reflection drops. Inquiry drops. Thinking becomes more passive. That changes how people handle information and each other.

AI talk focuses on extremes. The genuine risks are quieter. AI models learn from existing data. They pick up the biases and assumptions in that data. They repeat patterns, not the truth. They often sound confident. But confidence is not proof. You get a fresh problem. Confident inaccuracy. If people trust that output without checking, errors will build up. Not all at once. Slowly. And those errors can be worse.

Shruti's biggest worry wasn't jobs. It was disconnection. We can be connected to everything but grounded in nothing. This isn't just theory. It's already happening. "We are becoming more connected through technology—and more disconnected from each other," Shruti asserts.

I've felt it too. More access. More reach. More conversations. But less depth. Less presence. Less clarity. That's the trade-off in acceleration.

When we talked about blockchain. Her tone shifted. She called it Hope. A response to broken trust. To opaque systems and centralized control. But hope is still ahead of reality. That creates friction.

Systems develop faster than people. Where systems and people diverge, technology moves by capability. People move by understanding. Those clocks rarely line up. You can build something that works on paper and still have it fail with real users. People don't use things the way designers expect. That gap is where systems break.

AI cuts friction. It speeds up processes and makes them easier. But friction matters. It forces engagement. It forces thought. It builds understanding. When friction vanishes, depth often goes too. That changes how people learn and think.

This part got personal. Before my four-month podcasting break in the winter of 2026, I was inside the acceleration. Moving with the flow. Producing. Engaging. Keeping pace. Not always reflecting.

The break gave me distance. Distance gave clarity. I saw movement versus meaning. Connection versus presence. Activity versus depth. It changed how I will show up for my platform in the future.

Something became clear to me after Shruti and I talked, though: scaled intelligence changes what intelligence is. Human intelligence is contextual. It's shaped by experience, memory, and environment. It's about how an answer forms and what it connects to.

Then I heard Shruti whisper something that resonated loudly in my head and in my heart, "Technology can change systems. It cannot change beliefs."

When systems scale intelligence, those features shift. AI does not experience a memory problem...or a spirituality problem. It does not carry memory the same way humans do. It does not attach meaning. It works through pattern recognition and probability. That lets it produce results fast and at scale. But it alters what those results mean.

We engage with the simulation of understanding, not understanding itself. The difference is subtle but important. When something looks intelligent, people often assume it has the depth of human thought. They assign meaning where there may only be structure. They assign intention where there may only be a pattern. Over time, that changes how people interpret things. Not overnight. Gradually.

There's another effect too. As systems get better, people hand off more responsibility. First, small stuff. Clarifications. Summaries. Then, interpretation, analysis, judgment. Next, decisions. Each step feels small. Reasonable. But together they shift us. From active engagement to passive reliance. From thinking to accepting. From questioning to trusting.

It's not necessity that drives this process. It's ease. When something is easier and faster, people use it. Not because it's better. But because it removes effort. Ease becomes one of the strongest forces shaping behavior. And repeated behavior becomes normal.

Shruti's point that "if we don't develop consciously, we will just adapt faster," holds true for me. Normal behavior is the basis of new systems. That's the trade-off. We gain speed and access. But we risk losing depth and engagement. We risk losing the process that makes understanding stick. That process matters. Understanding is not just getting an answer. It's how that answer changes you.

If AI removes that process, something else has to replace it. Otherwise, we get a lot of information and little understanding. We get quick responses and shallow reflections. We gain accessible knowledge and rare insights. This isn't rejecting AI. It's noticing the impact.

Every system brings tradeoffs. The more powerful the system, the bigger the tradeoffs. The question isn't whether we'll build these systems. We will. The question is whether we stay awake to what changes. Whether we see what we gain and what we give up.

If we don't notice, the shift happens quietly. And by the time we see it, it's already embedded.

After talking with Shruti, I didn't walk away thinking only about AI. I walked away, thinking about responsibility. We're not just building systems that serve us. We're building systems that shape us.

That means the question changes.

It's no longer: What do we build?

It's: Who do we become if we do?

Chapter 5—Tech-Infused Entrepreneurship

Jean Criss is an author, columnist, digital media-entrepreneur, tech innovator, and fashion designer who thrives on bringing engaging community, content development, emerging tech, and communications to life. A 5X author, 4X award-winning e-commerce, digital creator, fashion designer, and global leader to support emerging tech and women's empowerment.

Contact Jean for writing, speaking, and creative content engagements info@jeancrissmedia.com.

Podcast Guest: Jean Criss
Podcast Date: April 11, 2025, Season 8
Podcast Link:
https://open.spotify.com/episode/7kBeC6KGiVbef JyTZliWXv?si=AkPTqXjyT7qhhfy6mUs8Jg

Some people choose entrepreneurship. Others are pushed into it.

That difference matters more than people think. When you choose it, you follow a vision, an idea of what could be. When you're pushed, you follow necessity.

Necessity creates a different builder.

I didn't get that at first. I pictured entrepreneurship as ambition, ideas, and wanting more. But over time, and after my break, I saw it starts differently for many people. Not with a plan. With disruption.

I heard "wanting more" in my talk with Jean Criss. Her path wasn't linear. Not clean. Not planned how most expect their entrepreneurship journey will go.

Her background? Computer science. Next, communications. Technology. Then media and advertising. On paper it looks like pivots. In real life, it was layers of experience.

Jean says, "I think it has come full circle... sometimes you have to explore different areas." Exploring doesn't always feel useful. It can feel scattered, even wasteful. But it compounds. Over time, you build the ability to see connections others miss.

Jean didn't stay in one lane. She built across the lanes. Media. Technology. Fashion. Publishing. Not separate projects. Interconnected systems.

That becomes an advantage later. Rarely obvious while you're in it.

Suddenly, everything changed. She was laid off. Soon after, she was diagnosed with breast cancer. Within thirty days, she started her business.

That was not strategy. That was survival. I can empathize...I discovered Bitcoin only after I was laid off from AIG in 2017. I learned how to invest in "altcoins" other than Bitcoin in 2019, only after two heart attacks at the end of 2018. And I learned how to become a podcaster in 2021, during the early days of my desmoid tumor journey. Jean "didn't wait for the right moment. I built with what I had."

Survival sharpens focus. You stop asking what the best idea is. You ask what you already have and how to use it. A different starting point. Most people wait. For timing. For certainty. For the right idea.

Builders like Jean don't have that luxury. They move with what exists. They assemble. They adapt. They build.

That mindset hit me harder than I expected. You stop looking outward and start looking inward. What do I know? What have I lived through? What can I build from here?

That shift from hunting opportunities to embracing reality changes everything. When Jean calls herself a "tech-infused entrepreneur," it's not branding. It's how she operates. She moves between domains.

And that's where the opportunity is now. At the intersections. Where systems touch. Where industries overlap.

Jean's work shows that. Media into fashion, then wearable tech. Storytelling and infrastructure. Idea into execution. But what stood out wasn't only the things she built. It was what she had to navigate.

Entrepreneurship is not clean. Not linear. Rarely controlled. It is chasing payments that never arrive. Managing partnerships that don't hold. Making decisions without full information. Taking risks without guarantees. "I'm still chasing $100,000 worth of business." That line cuts through the glossy version. It shows the part that doesn't get marketed or posted.

Entrepreneurship is pressure. Uncertainty. Responsibility. Over time, that pressure forces change. Jean learned when to walk away. When to fire partners. When to stay lean instead of scaling too fast. She even draws on advice linked to Daymond John: "Don't get greedy. Grow in a way that you can sustain."

That sounds simple. It's not. Everything around you pushes you in the opposite direction.

Grow faster.
Scale bigger.
Do more.

I know firsthand that doing more does not mean doing better. It is usually quite the opposite.

But growth without structure creates fragility. Fragility increases risk. So, the skill she learned isn't just how to achieve growth. It's how to achieve controlled growth. That requires practicing discipline.

Then there's execution. This is where builders split from everyone else. Ideas are everywhere. Execution is rare.

Jean put it plainly: Concept. Structure. Go-to-market. Execution. The framework isn't the point. The repeatability is. Once you know the sequence, you can run it again. And again. "It becomes turnkey." That's how you keep operating in uncertainty. You rely on a process, not a single outcome.

Her current work shows that approach.

Wearable tech is tied to health. Sensors that capture real-world data. Systems that use blockchain for integrity. This is where the space is moving. Away from narrative, toward utility.

She also reframed AI in a way that caught my attention. "Look at AI as your co-founder." Not a replacement. Leverage. An extension. People who adapt to AI won't resist it. They will integrate it. Jean does not see herself playing a static role; she sees herself as a dynamic builder. I see her that way, too.

Jean made a logical point. There's a gap between how entrepreneurship is described and how it really feels. From the outside, it looks like momentum. Idea, launch, growth, visibility. People focus on outcomes. The product that gains traction. The most successful narrative creates the most success.

Inside, it feels different. Not linear. Not controlled. Not stable. Jean is the part that doesn't get highlighted. The part that shows up when things go wrong. When payments don't come. When partners fall through. When timing is against you. When you must decide without full information and then live with those choices.

That reality changes how you operate. You stop thinking about perfect execution. You think about adaptability. You ask different questions. Not what's the best possible outcome, but what can I do with what I have now? "Entrepreneurship isn't about ideas; it's about execution." That shift separates people who talk about building from people who build.

There's also personal responsibility. When you build alone, the system and the person are the same. Decisions land immediately. They affect your time, your energy, your money (most definitely your money, or soon after, the lack thereof), and your ability to keep going.

Over time, you develop a different discipline. Not routine. Continuation. The ability to move forward when progress is uneven, when outcomes are unclear, and when things fail. Most people miss that. Building isn't just creativity. It's endurance.

Jean's story is about operating through uncertainty, adjusting when things change, walking away when something no longer works, staying lean when growth adds more risk than stability. Growth is often the goal. But growth without structure makes things fragile. The real challenge is to grow in a way that lasts.

One reality that gets too little attention is what it means to carry everything yourself. Inside a large company, responsibility is spread amongst multiple teams and stakeholders. Decisions are shared. Departments and processes act as buffers. Failures hit the system first, not the person.

When you're solo, none of that exists.

No buffer.

No separation.

Every choice carries weight.

Real consequences: financial, emotional, operational.

Your decisions shape the business and your ability to continue. That pressure compounds. At first, it looks obvious. Long hours. Uncertainty. Inconsistent results. Later it becomes internal. It changes how you think. How fast you move. How you decide.

There is no clean reset. You carry every outcome. Successes. Mistakes. Misjudgments. It accumulates. It forces you to be more aware and deliberate. Not to slow down for the sake of it, but because you know what happens when you move without clarity.

I've experienced this too, in the 2017 initial coin offering days of the cryptocurrency market. I had an advisory business where I kept changing my focus to keep up with regulatory clarity that kept changing, what seemed, as often as the wind was blowing. I shifted myself so much...I shifted myself right out of business and right into two heart attacks.

There's also isolation. Not being physically alone, but carrying responsibility in a way that others do not. People can advise and support each other. They are not carrying the same weight. That weight matters. It changes how choices feel. This is where endurance becomes more than persistence. It becomes stability.

It helps to shape your ability to operate while holding uncertainty and responsibility, and to decide without guarantees. Jean's experience shows that. Not just what she built, but how she kept going through disruption, health issues, and business uncertainty. She didn't just create something. She sustained herself while building it. That's a critical difference.

Building is usually framed as creation. The truth is all about continuation. Keeping going when conditions are bad, when outcomes are slow, and when progress isn't straight. That needs something other than skill. It needs capacity. The ability to absorb pressure without breaking. To adjust without losing direction. To continue without immediate payoff.

Most people don't see that. From the outside, they see movement, activity, and results. They don't see what it takes to sustain those things. I realized this while looking at my path. For a long time, I underplayed that layer. I thought in terms of output, visibility, and forward motion. Not enough about sustainability. Yet sustainability decides whether something lasts. Not how fast it starts. Not how visible it becomes. Whether it can continue under pressure. What I heard Jean say, and this is the sustainable message to me, at least, is, "Do not get greedy. Grow in a way that you can sustain."

That's the shift. Once you get it, you stop optimizing for momentum. You optimize for durability instead.

For the longest time, I chased output. Produce more. Stay active. Maintain presence.

But building something that lasts asks for something else.

Selectivity.
Restraint.
Awareness.

Knowing when to move and when to remain intact, building isn't about what you begin.

It's about what you can keep going.

Chapter 6—Nationalizing Digital Currencies

Tristan Thoma is Managing Director at Impera Strategy

Tristan led the implementation of the first and only operating national crypto system in the world in El Salvador. His firsthand experience in system and business design, technical architecture, and policy creation applies to both creative high-level strategic initiatives and the execution of precise tactical decisions. Working throughout the Americas, Europe, Asia, Africa, and the Middle East, Tristan has built over two dozen blockchain-integration models for Fortune 500 companies, governments, and startups. His current focus is supporting governments and financial institutions in developing national digital currencies to increase financial inclusion and resilience.

Since 2016, Tristan has pioneered innovative strategic solutions for the private and public sector implementing blockchain and advanced technology. Working throughout the Americas, Africa, Asia and Europe, he has led executive blockchain strategy for Fortune 500 companies and startups for industries including Banking, Payments, Asset Management, Supply Chain, IOT, Biotech, Transportation, Gaming, Agriculture, Real Estate and Trading.

With a background in Organizational Psychology and IT Systems Management, Tristan bridges the gap between technology and sustainable, human-centric design. He is passionate about Blockchain's potential for social impact and sustainability. Tristan is an avid speaker at Universities and conferences around the world.

Podcast Guest: Tristan Thoma
Podcast Date: June 9, 2025, Season 8

Podcast Link:
https://open.spotify.com/episode/57i5bUCU4Nx5
QDxEUVjV4h?si=j1evWAeLRGmWdPvzgjkF6w

****

At some point, ideas stop being enough. Because
eventually everything runs into the same question,
especially in cryptocurrency and blockchain:

Can this actually work?

That's where most things break.

Not at the level of vision. Not at the theoretical
level. At the level of reality.

I've seen that gap repeatedly. In crypto, in business,
and in systems more broadly. There's a difference
between what sounds interesting and what
legitimately functions when people use it. Between
what we think should happen and what happens

once incentives and things like regulation, culture, greed, and an assortment of habits (some good and some not good) show up.

That's what I was listening for when I spoke with Tristan Thoma. I did not listen for shiny new ideas. Not narratives either. Proof.

Tristan didn't start in finance or tech. He started in mindfulness and teaching kids. He worked directly with people. Immediate, tangible, deeply human. That matters a great deal because it shapes intent. He didn't enter the space because markets were hot or because blockchain sounded cool. He cared about impact and then hit the limit of doing that one person at a time. He wanted to do something on a much larger scale.

At some point, that becomes unavoidable. You can reach dozens directly. Maybe hundreds. But to reach millions, you need systems. That's where technology matters. Not as an abstraction, but as a multiplier. "People don't adopt technology because they believe in it. They adopt it because it works."

For Tristan, blockchain mattered because it changed the structure of trust. He didn't frame it the usual way. No ideology. No anti-establishment rhetoric. He focused on incentives. "This is an egalitarian technology. It aligns incentives."

That word, alignment, is everything. Systems rarely fail because people are dumb or evil. They fail because the incentives inside them produce distorted, extractive, or unstable outcomes. People respond to their environment. If the system rewards short-term moves, people act in the short-term. If it rewards opacity, people hide. If it rewards misalignment, misalignment spreads.

Tristan wanted to see what happens when incentives are set up differently. Blockchain, at its best, lets rules be encoded, execution automated, and trust shifted away from pure institutional dependence into system design. He put it plainly. "Blockchain becomes the third-party society never had."

That resonated with me because it reaches beyond software. Historically, trust depended on intermediaries such as banks, governments, legal structures, and institutions. Those systems can work. Often, they do. But they add friction, cost, and delay. And they have their own incentives.

Working at AIG for many years in my early corporate career, I saw how the effects of poorly written legislation led to tens of thousands of layoffs across corporate America in the 2010s. Executive incentives written into law rewarded the disparity between executive compensation and employee salaries. The larger the disparity...the higher the executive bonuses. That misalignment drove me to the crypto industry. Tristan reminded me of that.

Blockchain changes where trust sits. It doesn't remove institutions entirely. It lets some functions move from human discretion into system design. Sounds elegant in theory. But the gap between elegant theory and real-world implementation is where things break.

And that is where Tristan works. Through Impera Strategy, he operates where most in crypto don't: governments, institutions, regulated environments, and national systems. That is not the same as building a token, launching a protocol, or publishing an unqualified opinion thread online about the future. It's slower, messier and harder.

It's also more revealing, because once tech hits the real world, it must survive contact with reality. That reality includes infrastructure limitations, laws, culture, public trust, institutional inertia, and political pressure. Not talking about edge cases here. Rather, the complete environment.

Any system that can't function within that environment isn't an actual system yet. It's still a concept.

That distinction matters because so much in crypto still lives at the conceptual level. We will talk about what could be possible. We will talk about disruption and the future. But we don't always talk about translation, which is how a system moves from concept to adoption, from design to behavior, and from possibility to use.

Tristan's examples were grounded in that translation layer. These examples include:

- Systems to fight modern slavery by keeping workers' identities and contracts under their control instead of letting employers hold those documents.
- Systems that let farmers store grain, tokenize it and sell over time so they aren't forced into seasonal price pain.

These are not speculative use cases. They are practical. They deal with real constraints in tough environments with very high stakes. That's when the blockchain conversation gets serious. Not when we ask what it could theoretically replace. But when we ask what can be improved in actual conditions.

When we talked about El Salvador, Tristan cleared up something that's often misunderstood. The public story is usually that Bitcoin became the national currency, and everything changed overnight. That's not the real lesson. The real lesson is practical. Bitcoin was added as a tool, not shoved in as a total replacement. That matters because it shows how adoption works in real life.

People don't adopt systems for ideology alone. They adopt them when they are useful in context. Faster. Cheaper. More accessible. Easier to use for a specific problem. That's how adoption happens. Not through sweeping abstraction, but through practical advantage.

That changed how I think about crypto's future. It's not mostly a story of total replacement. It's a story of integration. Less dramatic. Less cinematic. Less satisfying if you want a revolution. But more realistic if you care about outcomes.

Realism is something Tristan brings into focus. He doesn't frame crypto and traditional finance as enemies. He said something many still struggle to say: "I am a fan of Bitcoin, and I am a fan of banks."

Not a contradiction.

Maturity.

Both systems serve different functions. Crypto offers sovereignty, portability, and programmability, and sometimes access where none exists. Banks offer structure, recourse, and familiar trust. Most people don't want to live only in one world. They want benefits from both.

Therefore, the future will probably look hybrid. Not purely centralized. Not purely decentralized.

Layered. Contextual. Selective.

That's why his work in places like Bolivia matters. Building regulatory frameworks, linking institutions to decentralized infrastructure, and creating ways to adopt without forcing people to abandon the old world overnight.

Systems develop that way. Not clean breaks, but transitional architecture. One thing became obvious after this conversation. Execution at scale differs significantly from execution in isolation. Building in a controlled environment is one thing. Deploying into a world of unstable variables, misaligned stakeholders, incomplete infrastructure, and low trust is another.

That's where most systems fail. Not because they don't work technically, but because they don't translate behaviorally. Behavioral translation matters more than most technologists want to admit.

There's a recurring assumption that if something is technically better, it will be adopted. It doesn't work that way. People don't adopt things because they are elegant. They adopt them when they are legible, usable and trustworthy in their lives. Thus, implementation must cover stuff that doesn't show up in technical specifications or, as was popular for a long time in crypto...whitepapers.

Fear, habit, confusion, cultural expectations, institutional trust, and how willing people are to change behavior for an unclear future benefit matter more. Those are big reasons why education matters in adoption. The biggest barrier is often not the tool. It's understanding. How to use it. How to manage risk. How to recover from mistakes. How to tell if a system is trustworthy or just new.

When financial systems change, behavior changes with them, and behavior is harder to change than code. That ties directly to why Tristan's work matters.

He's not at the level of possibility. He's at the layer of usability. Where design must meet human behavior and still work.

There's another layer you notice when you look at systems this way. The weight of the consequences. In the real world, stakes change. You are not dealing with isolated outcomes. Decisions affect communities, institutions, and markets. Failure doesn't stay boxed. It spreads. That creates a different responsibility.

You think less about isolated success and more about systemic impact. You ask second-order questions:

- If this works, what changes downstream?
- If it fails, who absorbs the cost?
- If it scales, what pressure appears elsewhere?

This is the point where blockchain stops being a novelty and starts becoming infrastructure. Infrastructure is not interesting because it's new. It matters because people rely on it. Reliance changes the moral weight of implementation.

I will always remember that. In crypto, we often pretend systems exist in isolation. They don't. Every financial rail, every identity layer, every tokenized asset, every regulatory choice sits inside a broader social structure.

Once something touches that structure, you are no longer just building software. You are shaping the conditions. That's why the line "we are not forcing adoption; we are enabling choice" matters so much.

Choice is the right framework. Not because it sounds softer, but because it respects how systems evolve. Useful systems spread when they offer an advantage. Durable systems endure when they improve outcomes without demanding total ideological conversion.

That idea changed how I think about progress. Progress is often framed as breakthroughs, disruption, and speed. But genuine progress, especially where money and identity are involved, is usually quieter. Integration. Optionality. Paths people can take. "You don't replace systems overnight. You integrate into them."

After speaking with Tristan, one thing became clearer. This space does not mostly need more ideas or more narratives. It needs people who can make complex systems work. Because the future will not be defined by what is theoretically possible. It will be defined by what works. And the people who can close the gaps between idea and execution, technology and adoption, and theory and consequence, are the ones who shape what comes next.

That is what Tristan represents. Not the loudest voice in the room. Not the most ideological. But one of the most necessary: the builder who asks not whether something sounds transformative, but whether it survives contact with reality.

In the end, that may be the question that matters most.

Chapter 7—The Signal That Remains

There is a quiet, often unremarkable moment when everything changes.

That moment doesn't announce itself. There is no ceremony. There are no audiences. And you receive no recognition.

It is not the moment you set out for it to be. Nor is it the moment you arrive. It's somewhere in-between, when the noise fades just enough. Where uncertainty meets the need for faith. Where fear is in the mirror looking squarely back at you, and you decide to move your energy differently to embrace the uncertainty.

You hear something that was always there:

The signal.

I didn't recognize it at first. Not when I left my early career, sold everything I owned and set out for Asia. Not when I moved through countries, landscapes, versions of myself I didn't yet understand. Not even when I came back, whether it be when I began a new corporate career, met my wife and started a family, or joined the cryptocurrency industry.

I only recognized it when all my movement stopped. When I stepped away from podcasting and from being caught up in the algorithms of social media that painted a different version of the world—a much darker version of the world—than what I believe in. When the world of information, news, and noise got smaller. When quiet moments outside in the winter became something entirely different inside of me.

If anything, the signal only got clearer when everything else internally grew louder. The diagnosis. My uncertainty. The physical toll.

Quiet moments weren't peaceful but heavy. The shift from forward motion to forced stillness, which forced me to re-examine my purpose. The life I thought I was building paused. The identity I thought I knew as the Crypto Hipster, churning out episode after episode, was challenged.

And yet, under it all, something whispered quietly in my ear. It was not loud. Not obvious. But steady. The signal was never in continuous movements. Not in travel, conversation, or the pile of experiences. Not in the podcast, the interviews, or the hundreds of voices I had the privilege of speaking with.

The signal was in the pattern.

Patterns show up when you step back far enough to see them. When I started the Crypto Hipster Podcast, I was chasing curiosity. I talked to anyone building, anyone thinking, anyone willing to share their story. Over time, those conversations added up. Hundreds of them. Different people, different backgrounds, different ideas. On the surface, it looked like noise. Different projects. Different narratives. Different visions of what this space could be.

But over time, things repeated themselves. Not the details. The intent underneath.

And that is what this book is about. Not just the stories. The signal that runs through them.

Nikhil talked about systems, not as fixed things but as living frameworks that change when people join. The architecture itself is not nearly as important as the idea behind it. Technological coordination itself can be redesigned. How people organize, decide, and act together isn't fixed. It's a choice.

That is a signal.

It pushes back against the idea that the systems we inherit are the only ones we can have.

Shruti came at it from a trust, data, and identity perspective...a human perspective. While Nikhil looked at coordination, she looked at verification.

How do we know what's true, who controls that truth, and how it could be structured to serve people instead of institutions?

Another signal.

Why? Because under the tech talk was a bigger question: Who owns reality in a digital world?

Jean brought something different: a bridge between technology and people. Between ideas and proper use. And between technology and the failures and mistakes learned in entrepreneurship. Her work wasn't just about what could be built. It was about who would help, and how systems move from abstract to real impact, especially where the stakes are human, immediate, and personal.

Another signal.

Jean reminds us that technology, at best, is not about technology itself, but about what it enables. It's about how to make this blockchain thing, this AI thing, this amorphous conceptual thing, human.

And Tristan directly cut through things with sharp clarity. Markets, incentives, decision-making, and the notion that instead of leaning on centralized authority or fixed governance, we can create systems where outcomes come from participation, aligned incentives, and collective intelligence shown through action.

Another signal.

Innovation reframes authority. And it is not something handed down, but something that emerges. Four conversations. Four domains. Four ways of seeing the world.

But the same pattern: a move away from centralized control. A move toward individual agency. A belief that systems can and should be rebuilt.

Now, this is where the signal turns personal. Nothing matters if it stays "out there." It's easy to talk about decentralization as an idea. But it is much harder to live it. It is so easy to talk about agency in the abstract, but it is much harder to take responsibility for your own direction when the path is unclear. It is easy to admire builders, but harder to become one.

I'm a builder, too. Mostly, my life and how I see myself and my role in the world. Once destined for jails, institutions or death—just like anyone with severe, hopeless alcohol addiction ends up—I walk a free man. Once destined to be a statistic in Kathmandu during the rainy season, I live to tell the story of my journey home. And once confronted with my mortality and morbidity, I walk in faith that God is present in my long-life adventure to come.

My journey started as movement across the world; it became something else. The physical journey ended. The internal one didn't. Coming back. Starting again. Rebuilding in a smaller space. Facing limits I didn't pick. Letting go of versions of myself that no longer fit.

No narrative glamor in that. No highlight reel. Just the quiet, steady choice to keep going.

And that, more than anything, is the signal.

Not the big ideas. Not the frameworks. Not the tech. But the decision, repeatedly, to move forward.

If there's one thing that links every builder, every founder, every person on this path, it isn't certainty.

Nor is it clarity. And it is not being successful materially.

It is the willingness to act without guarantees. To build without permission. To continue without recognition.

The noise will always be there. Markets rise and fall. Narratives shift. Projects come and go. Voices get loud, then vanish. None of that is the signal.

The signal is quieter.

It is created by the person who keeps building when no one watches. Not the critic. Not the influencer. Not the diva. Rather, the individual who thinks for themselves when it would be easier to follow. The choice to create, to act, to join in without waiting for validation.

That's what I saw again and again across hundreds of conversations. Not identical ideas. Identical intent. A refusal to accept the world as it is. A belief that it can be shaped. And the willingness to shape it.

This book is not the ultimate answer. It is also not a noisy statement about where this space is going or what it will become.

It's a reflection: a snapshot of a time in my life when the signal is getting clearer, but it is still easy to miss.

Most people won't hear it. Not because they can't. But because it asks for something: attention, discipline, and patience to sit with uncertainty until clarity shows up.

For those who hear it, even faintly, things change. It changes how you see systems. It changes how you see opportunities. And it changes how you see yourself.

For me, it changed everything. Not all at once. Not in a dramatic sweep. But steadily. In how I think. In how I choose. In how I move forward.

The signal doesn't tell you what to do. There are no instructions. It doesn't come with a manual. There are no guarantees.

What it asks is simpler and harder: To make a decision.

And that is where it starts. Not in systems. Not in markets. Not in conversations. But in the individual. In you. In me. And in each of us.

If there is one thread from the first page to now, it is this: The signal is not "out there." It never was.

It's in the decision to keep going, no matter what. In the willingness to build. Knowing that while the world is loud, clarity is there for those who look and act on what they find.

Everything else is just volume. Everything else is just noise. And my aim is to recognize the signal through all the noise.

If you've made it this far, you've already done something most won't. You listened. Now the harder part starts.

What will you do with what you've heard?

Appendix A: About the Author

Jamil Hasan is the founder of Crypto Hipster Publications and host of the Crypto Hipster Podcast, a platform dedicated to one core idea: where builders talk freedom, not price.

Across over 580 interviews, he has focused on founders, entrepreneurs, and independent creators—the people actively building the digital economy from the ground up. His work is not about market cycles or short-term narratives, but about understanding the deeper motivations, risks, and convictions behind those creating new systems.

Jamil's approach is rooted in filtering signals from noise. In an industry often driven by speculation and surface-level commentary, he has built a platform that prioritizes long-term thinking, first-principles discussion, and authentic perspectives.

Before fully committing to the digital asset space, Jamil built his career across financial services and data-driven initiatives, including early-work connected to blockchain, artificial intelligence, and client-facing strategy. That foundation informs his ability to translate complex technological change into clear, human insights.

After stepping away from his work during a period of intensive medical treatment, he returned with a sharper lens and a more defined mission: to elevate real builders, challenge conventional narratives, and document the ideas shaping the future of the digital economy.

He returned with a sharper lens and a more defined mission: to elevate real builders, reject noise disguised as insight, and focus only on what endures.

Signals Through the Noise represents the next evolution of that mission.

Appendix B: Crypto Hipster's Curtain Calls Episodes

A complete list of Jamil's Crypto Hipster's Curtain Calls podcast compilations from Seasons 6-8 is presented below. These compilations set the basis and foundational groundwork for the current Crypto Hipster's book series. Each podcast episode, except for the first one, starts with a question, and each book answers that question. These episodes comprise fifty guests from Season 6, one hundred guests from Season 7, and one hundred thirty-one guests from Season 8.

All of them can be found at anchor.fm/crypto-hipster-podcast and can be listened to on Spotify, Apple Podcasts, Amazon, YouTube, Anchor, or wherever enjoy your favorite podcasts, including the full interviews from each of the guests presented in this book.

Ep. 1: Insights On Leadership, Sustainability, and the Global Digital Economy

Ep. 2: The Lost Message? How Crypto Is Still About Financial Freedom and Global Socio-Economic Betterment.

Ep. 3: Bitcoin: A Beauty or a Beast? Why Bitcoin and All Its Features Will Stand the Test of Time.

Ep. 4: FTX: The First of Many Crypto Implosions to Come? How We Can Overcome Additional Existential Challenges in Web3.

Ep. 5: People are People, so Why Should It Be? Intellectual Property Advancement Should Develop So Effortlessly in Web3.

Ep. 6: Sam's Coin? How Solana's Continued Development Has Strengthened Its Network and Transformed It Into Much More Than Just "Sam's Coin."

Ep. 7: A Dopamine Kick? How to Avoid Getting Obliterated When Chasing 10,000X.

Ep. 8: The Ghost in You? Seeing Yourself Through the Eyes of Decentralized AI.

Ep. 9: Our Independence Day? How Crypto Can Improve Our Daily Lives and Create Paths for Personal Freedom.

Ep. 10: Mercy, Mercy Me? Why We Should Advance Sustainability Initiatives Using Generational Decentralized Technology.

Ep. 11: Our Lips Are Sealed? Why We Should Think and Talk About a Future Filled With Helpful AI Agents.

Ep. 12: Gods of War? How to Navigate the Bitcoin Cycle Waves Proactively Without Running Riot.

Ep. 13: Peace of Mind? How to Break Free From Instant Dopamine Kicks and Make Solid, Long-Term Crypto Investing Choices.

Ep. 14: Land of Confusion? Helping Investors and Traders Navigate the Wild West of Cryptocurrencies.

Ep. 15: Bizarre Love Triangle? A Web3 Bill of Rights, Crypto's Good Ole Days, and the Three Magi of Blockchain.

Ep. 16: Another Day in Paradise? Why The OG Cryptocurrencies Need Saving and How a Bright Future Ought to Become Reality.

Ep. 17: Stairway to Heaven? Why We Are Climbing A Destined Pathway Toward a Fully Tokenized Future.

Ep. 18: More Than a Feeling? Re-imagining Sports Betting Through Decentralization.

Ep. 19: I Like to Move It, Move It? Sparking a Rapid Explosion of the Decentralized Entertainment Industry.

Ep. 20: Money for Nothing? Understanding the Future of Digital Currencies Beneath the Hype Hood.

Ep. 21: Groove Is in the Heart? How to Get Your Groove On by Using Artificial Intelligence Agents.

Ep. 22: Fields of Gold? How the Future of Bitcoin Shines Brightly Even When the Price Sometimes Drops to a Number Unsightly.

Ep. 23: Little Pink Houses for You and Me? How Independent Creators Can Trust the Crypto Industry Again.

Ep. 24: Eye in the Sky? Taking a World View of the Future of Digital Identity, E-Commerce, and Web3 File Storage.

Ep. 25: Wheel in the Sky? Focusing on the Fun Journey of Web3 Gaming.

Ep. 26: Blue Sky Action? How to Navigate the Complexities of Crypto Auditing, Accounting, and Financial Reporting.

Ep. 27: You Down With O.P.P.? Why Revolutionizing Blockchain Security Will Keep Others From Coveting and Stealing Your Property.

Ep. 28: Let's Make Lots of Money? Unlocking the Possibilities of Enriching the World Using Decentralized Finance Platforms and Protocols.

Ep. 29: The Grand Illusion? Why Ushering In a New World of AI Superintelligence is Much More a Reality Than an Illusion.

Ep. 30: Only Time Will Tell? Overcoming Hackers, Pandemics, and Identity Threats Through Unique Cryptographic Solutions.

Ep. 31: Only the Young? How to Make Decentralized Finance (DeFi) a Safe and Attractive Journey For All Generations To Benefit.

Ep. 32: We've Only Just Begun? How We Are Just In the Early Innings of the Global Decentralized Finance Evolution.

Ep. 33: Rain on the Scarecrow? How to Build Web3 Gaming Solutions That Sustain the Original Ethos of the Blockchain Industry & Bypass Bankers' Bloodthirsty Greed to Destroy It All.

Ep. 34: Two Tickets to Paradise? Why the Future of Non-Fungible Tokens is Bright Despite Having Troubles in Paradise.

Ep. 35: Dancing in the Dark? Why Many Crypto Founders Are Fumbling Around In the Dark Regarding Global Crypto Regulations and What They Can Do About It.

Ep. 36: That Was Yesterday? How to Implement Forward-Looking Regulatory Solutions to Some of the Industry's Greatest Challenges.

Ep. 37: I've Got the Power? How Web3 Can Help Content Creators Regain Ownership Over Their Personal Content and Grasp the Power Back From Big Tech Firms That Seek to Exploit Them.

Ep. 38: Ain't We Funkin' Now? How Blockchain Technology, Through Innovation and Education, Are Causing Breakthroughs in Some Funky-Cool Markets.

Ep. 39: In the Name of Love? They Can Try to Take Away Our Crypto, But They Cannot Take Away Our Pride.

Ep. 40: Why Can't This Be Love? Why Passion and Social Impact Remain at the Heart of Web3 Development.

Ep. 41: Don't Come Around Here No More? Why Leveraging Blockchain Technology to Make a Difference for Humanity Continues to and Always Will Matter Most.

Ep. 42: Home By The Sea? Why Decentralized Finance is Primed to Outperform Traditional Finance Even During the Most Turbulent Tides.

Ep. 43: Sultans of Swing? Empowering Crypto Traders and Investors with Useful Tools and Opportunities to Take Full Advantage of Their Web3 Experiences.

Ep. 44: 1979? While Artificial Intelligence is Nothing New, How We Harness Its Power Has Transformed Dramatically In the Last Half-Century.

Ep. 45: Walking on the Moon? Leveraging AI Models to Transform Amorphous Ethical Ideals Into Solid Earthly Business Practices.

Ep. 46: 2000 Light-Years From Home?
Courageously Exploring the Impending Universal
Explosion of Real-World Tokenized Assets.

Ep. 47: Every Rose Has Its Thorn? Despite a
Thorny Path Thus Far, Why the Future of
Blockchain Development is On An Increasingly
Smoother Road Heading Toward Tomorrow.

Ep. 48: Another Brick in the Wall? Why
Blockchains Must Be Implemented Brick by Brick
Globally for Everyone's Benefit.

Ep. 49: Boogie Wonderland? How
Programmable Decentralized Money Will Help Us
All Embark Upon Creating a Self-Sovereign,
Trusted Web3 World.

Ep. 50: Boogie Nights? Learning Life Lessons
and Web3 Trading Strategies From Crypto's Role in
Liquor, Laundering, Lust, and Luxury.

Ep. 51: The Sky is Crying? How Web3 Financial
Engineering Has Altered the Purpose and Vision of
Blockchain Technology From Idealistic Altruism to
Profit Maximization.

Ep. 52: Invisible Touch? How to Fend Off Your
Inner Demons While Trading Cryptocurrencies by
Using Automation Tools, Security Measures, and
Risk Management Techniques.

Ep. 53: A Touch of Grey? How the Power of Blockchain and Web3 Extends to Even the Most Illiquid Markets and Grayest Areas of Investing.

Ep. 54: Out of Touch? Why Transforming On-Chain Compute Into Real World Tangible Assets is Not Such a Remote and Distant Possibility.

Ep. 55: Thunderstruck? How Zero-Knowledge Strikes Open the Chasm Separating a New, Abundant Decentralized Future from the Ancient and Nearly Extinct Traditional Financial System.

Ep. 56: Welcome to the Jungle? How to Navigate What Lurks in the Jungle of Decentralized Finance Successfully.

Ep. 57: Wanted Dead or Alive? Why We Should Stop Listening to Critics Who Falsely Pronounce Bitcoin's Death, and Focus Instead on Building an Open, Collaborative, Better Society.

Ep. 58: Mainstreet? How Wall Street's "Bitcoin Capture" Robbed Main Street Investors and What We Can Do About It.

Ep. 59: Rock of Ages? Why Crypto Has Been Resilient Through Multiple Storms Despite Threats From Every Direction and Evil Forces Trying to Destroy It.

Ep. 60: Peaceful Easy Feeling? How to Overcome Systemic Challenges So Traders and

Investors Can Confidently and Serenely Navigate the Crypto Market.

Ep. 61: Shiny Happy People? How Crypto Has Created a New Class of Economic Survivors and Affluent Outcasts From the Traditional Financial System and Social Networks.

Ep. 62: Heaven's On Fire? How Decentralized Infrastructure's Evolution Sparked the Inferno to Burn Bridges to the Ground and Build an Inclusive World for Financial Freedom.

Ep. 63: Fire and Rain? Unifying Fragmented Economies to Introduce the Next Billion Users to the Web3 World.

Ep. 64: We Didn't Start the Fire? Why Blockchain's Evolution Is More Important Than Greedy Bankers & Crooked Politicians Making a Quick Buck for Themselves at Your Expense.

Ep. 65: Edge of Seventeen? How the Failures and Successes of the 2017 Initial Coin Offering Era Led to Later Advancements in Cryptographic Innovation.

Ep. 66: Bitter Sweet Symphony? How Enduring the Growing Pains of a Nascent Web3 Industry Today Will Lead to a Thriving Global Economy Tomorrow.

Ep. 67 (FINALE): Jump? Taking the Leap Out From the Pains of the Old World and Into the Joys of the Web3 Future.

Appendix C: Crypto Hipster Podcasts

A complete list of Jamil's Crypto Hipster Podcasts from Seasons 6-8 is presented below. All of them can be found at anchor.fm/crypto-hipster-podcast and can be listened to on Spotify, Apple Podcasts, Amazon, YouTube, Anchor, or wherever enjoy your favorite podcasts, including the full interviews from each of the guests presented in this book.

This appendix lists Seasons 6, 7, and 8 podcasts by category and genre. For Seasons 1 through 5, please check out some of my Crypto Hipster Chronicles and Crypto Hipster Mysticals books and compilations, or listen to my podcasts at Crypto Hipster wherever you listen to your favorite podcasts.

Accounting and Finance for Cryptocurrencies

- How to Best Navigate the Complexities of Crypto Accounting, with Rich Zhou @ Aquifer CFO

- Building a CPA Firm That Not Only Understands Digital Assets But Also Serves as a Trustworthy Strategic Partner for Web3 Businesses, with Patrick Camuso @ Camuso CPA

- Creating Consistency, Consensus, and Auditing Standards Across the World of Blockchain Technology, with Hind Kurhan @ Thesis* Defense

- Designing Trusted Environments to Drive Mass Adoption of On-Chain Finance, with Jeff Owens @ Haven1

Creating Artificial Intelligence Agents

- Building a Decentralized Platform Where Anyone Can Create Their Own Custom AI Agents, with Colin Fitzpatrick @ Griffin AI

- Exploring the Future of AI Agents and Their Applications for Decentralized Finance and Banking, with Bullet Bulat @ ReDeFi

- Pioneering the Creation of Emotionally Intelligent AI Companions and the First IP-Powered AI Protocol, with Max Giammario @ Kindred

- Building an On-Chain Arena to Reward the Best AI Agents, with Andrew Hill @ Recall

- How to Design Decentralized Infrastructures That Make Artificial Intelligence Agents Reliable, with Karan Sirdesai @ Mira Network

- Making AI Accessible Through Community-Driven Data Training, with Johanna Rose Cabildo @ Data Guardians Network (D-GN)

- Tapping Into a Global Contributor Network to Source AI Verified Insights, with Rowan Stone @ Sapien

- Movement in Action!: How Personal Customized AI Agents Can Help Improve

Your Health and Catapult the Movement Economy, with Oleg Fomenko @ SWEAT

AI Modeling

- One Hundred Years of Artificial Intelligence and Its Future with the Intersection of Blockchain Technology, with Dr. Alok Aggarwal @ Scry AI

- Why We Should Create a Collaborative AI-Powered Blockchain Economy That Benefits Everyone, with Sean Ren @ Sahara Labs

- Discovering the Dolcelorian, an AI Agent Uniquely Suited for a Platform Rebellion, with Justin Banon @ Boson Metasystem

- Crypto Hipster Podcast Episode 300. A Vision for Change through the Eyes of AI, with Paulius Stankevicius

- 2024 Holiday Special: Why Preventing Theft and Fraud By Using AI in Crypto Matters, with Michal "Mehow" Pospieszalski @ MatterFi

- Ushering in a New World of Sovereign Superintelligence, with Ahmad Shadid @ O.xyz

- Building AI 3.0 to Overcome Systemic Challenges Within the Web3 Industry, with Chen Feng @ Autonomys

- Exploring the Intersection of Human-Generated Data, Blockchain, and Artificial Intelligence, with Kurt Ivy @ HumanizedAI

- How to Architect a Decentralized Global Data Marketplace for the AI Era, with Brendan Playford @ Masa

- Creating Scalable Infrastructures and Decentralized Systems That Reward AI Model Creators, with Erick Ho @ Function Network

- Harnessing the Power of Artificial Intelligence and Machine Learning to Change the Game and Transform the World, with Wei Xie @ ArenaX Labs

- Crypto Hipster Presents: Reporter on the Ground, Episode 10: Pioneering Advancements in Secure, Collaborative AI Model Training and Deployment, with Jiahao Sun @ FLock.io

- How to Harness the Power of High-End GPUs for Scalable and Efficient AI Model Training, with Jakub Ondrášek @ Clore.AI

- How to Democratize 3-D Content Creation With Advancements in AI Architecture, with Ben James @ 404-GEN

- Unifying Access to Top DeFi Protocols That Secures Capital Deployment Into Decentralized AI, with Yaroslav Writtle @ Yelay

- Examining the Importance of Transparency and Verification in AI Decision-Making Processes, with Jason Teutsch @ Truebit

Bitcoin

- How to Make Bitcoin Transactions Safe, Simple, and Accessible for Everyone, with Sung Choi @ Coinme

- Why Bitcoin Is Unbreakable in the Face of Black Swan Global Events, with Agne Linge @ WeFi

- Crypto Hipster Presents: Shooting from the Hip, Episode 1: The Meaning and Beauty of Bitcoin Maximalism, with Vlad Costea @ Bitcoin Takeover Podcast

- Bitcoin & Beyond: Pioneering Innovation in the Crypto Payments Industry with Mark Højgaard @ Coinify

- Why the Next Crypto Winter and a Bitcoin Price Drop to $60K Is Now in the Cards, with Clem Chambers @ aNEWfn.com

- How to Ride the Bitcoin Halving Wave Using Investing Techniques Everyone Should Know, with Edward Mehrez @ Arrow Markets

- Why Bitcoin-Native Xapo Bank Members Are Using Bitcoin as a Retirement Investment Product, with Seamus Rocca @ Xapo Bank

- Ordinals, Optionality, and Taking a Pragmatic Approach to Building Out the Bitcoin Mining Stack, with Sheldon Bennett and Steven Eliscu @ DMG Blockchain Solutions

- How to Build a Tax-Free Retirement Nest Egg With Self-Directed Bitcoin IRAs, with Adam Bergman, Esq. @ IRA Financial

- Crypto Hipster Presents...Shooting from the Hip!, Episode 7: Solving the Misaligned Incentive Strategies with Bitcoin and Ethereum, with David Lancashire @ Saito

- How Bitcoin Ordinals Can Pave the Way for Individual "Tokenized" On-Chain Identities and Financial Inclusion Globally, with Taha Abbasi @ Ferrum Network

- Bitcoin 3.0: Developing the Next Evolutionary Phase of the Bitcoin Ecosystem, with Rajiv Khemani @ Auradine

Blockchain Implementation

- Onboarding the Next Wave of Developers into Web3 and Supporting Them to Build Intelligent Infrastructures, with Johnny @ Empyreal SDK

- Why Now Is the Best Time to Build Infrastructure That Fosters the Development of Institutional Financial Systems on the Bitcoin Blockchain Network, with Vakeesan Mahalingam @ Torram

- Pioneering the Future of Digital Asset Management and Blockchain Integration, with Darren Carvalho @ MetaWealth

- Increasing Intelligence, Understanding Money, and Developing a Customer-Centric Approach to Building Your Web3 Business, with Cyrus Taghehchian @ SHOPX

- Why Polkadot's Ambassador Program Will Help Create a Bright Future for Blockchain Developers, with Lucy Coulden @ Polkadot

- Empowering Developers to Build Compliant Web3 Applications That Protect User Privacy, with Joe Andrews @ Aztec Labs

- DAOs, "Dots", and the Future of Web Three Developers, with Bill Laboon @ Web3 Foundation

- Empowering Analysts and Developers to Query, Create, and Build the Future of Finance Using Proprietary Web 3 Data Algorithms, with Jim Myers @ Flipside Crypto

- Why Everyone Should Have Access to On-Chain Payments Across Multiple Blockchains, with Adrien Stern @ Reveel

- Helping Early-Stage Founders Leverage Blockchain Technology to Bring Forth Their Ventures to the World, with Aly Madhavji @ Blockchain Founders Fund

- How Simplifying Blockchain Access Helps Users Build "Whatever, Wherever", with Yair Cleper @ Magma Devs / Lava Network

- Creating a Richer and More Robust Blockchain Developer Space in Nigeria with a 4-Week Master Class, with Jathin Jagannath and Awoskia Israel Ayodeji

- Smart Contracts, Programmable Money, and Building an Interoperable Technology World, with Dr. Weijia Zhang @ Wanchain

- How to Connect the Global Crypto Ecosystem on One Platform, with Peter Kris @ Gasp

- Solving the Siloed Network Environment Problem to Embark Upon Building a Native, Decentralized, Multi-Chain, Web Three World, with Omer Sadika @ dWallet Labs

- Building Discreet Log Contracts To Create Trustless Bridges Between Bitcoin and Ethereum and Foster the Evolution of Decentralized Finance, with Aki Balogh @ DLC.Link

- How to Unify and Enhance Accessibility of Blockchain Data Across Various Networks, with Bunny @ DORA

- Building the World's First Layer-One Programmable Data Chain, with Josh Benaron @ Irys

- Building the Web3 Generation of "Amazon Web Services" through Cloud Service Providers, with Sebastian Pfeiffer @ Impossible Cloud Network

- How to Build an Open, Serverless, and Permissionless Compute Network that Drives Positive Change for a Global Society, with Alison Haire @ Lilypad

- Leveraging Crypto to Dissolve Barriers That Have Relegated the Unbanked and Under-banked to the Financial Sidelines, with Kathy Roberts @ Switch Reward Card

- Creating a New Class of Reactive Decentralized Web3 Applications on a Dream Computer, with John Vibes @ Somnia.Network

- Envisioning a Future Where Banks Embrace Blockchain Technology, with Lindsey Lim @ Radix Foundation

- How Based Roll-ups Can Help Even the Smallest Fish Swim Mightily in the Largest Pond, with Amir Forouzani @ Puffer Finance

- Unlocking the Future of Blockchain with Zero-Knowledge Proofs, with Teemu Päivinen @ ZkCloud

- Pioneering the World's First Super-Computer Powered by Handheld Devices, with Butian Li @ Bless Network

- Crypto Hipster Presents: Reporter on the Ground, Episode 5; Building Cryptographically Secure Cold Storage Facilities for Institutions, with Oliver von Landsberg-Sadie @ MPCH

- Building, Scaling and Developing Large-Scale Distributed Cloud Systems on the Blockchain Ground-Floor in Serbia, with Bogdan Habic @ Tenderly

- How to Empower the Automation of Day-to-Day Operations and Innovate Today Rather Than Months from Now, with William Herkelrath @ K3 Labs

- How to Help Web3 Developers Easily Deploy Hybrid dApps on Telegram, with Pavel Altukhov @ TAC

- Advancing the Technical Frontier and Evolution of the NEAR Protocol, with Bowen Wang @ NEAR One

- How to Create a Thriving Prediction App System On-Chain, with Dan Kaizer @ Azuro

- Crypto Hipster Presents: Reporter on the Ground, Episode 4; Why Disaster Recovery Processes are a Critical Component of Building Crypto Custody Infrastructures, with Haden Patrick @ Cordial Systems

- How to Empower Decentralized Order Book Exchanges with Tim Wang @ Elixir

- Unlocking the Full Potential of Blockchain by Creating the First Universal Layer Two Protocol with Native Restaking, with Karan Bharadwaj @ Arithmic

- Why Decentralized Physical Infrastructure Networks are blockchain's next big trend, with Michael O'Rourke @ Pocket Network

Blockchain Security

- Exploring the Benefits of Revolutionizing Blockchain Security Measures that Protect Us from Key Exploits, with Riad Wahby @ Cubist

- Crypto Hipster Presents...Shooting from the Hip! E14: How Creating Robust Economic Security Helps to Fend Off Even the Strongest Adversaries and Weakest Protocol Security Infrastructures w/ Dan Hughes

- Creating a Universal Web Three Privacy Encryption Layer to Secure the Decentralized World, with Julian Deschler @ Elusiv

- When Does the Bull Run? Crypto and Blockchain Security Insights for the Upcoming Bull Market, with Hexens

- How White Hat Hackers Are Transforming Web Two Cyber Security Initiatives to a Web Three Future, with Sipan Vardanyan and Vahe Karapetyan @ Hexens

- Reimagining Blockchain Security and Multi-Party Computing with an Innovative Approach to Building Digital Asset Networks, with Michael Cunningham @ io.finnet

- How to Create Bespoke Solutions that Solve New Identity Threats Posed by Artificial Intelligence and Bots, with Kitty Horlick @ Rarify Labs (Part 1 of 2)

- Global Pandemics, EMP Threats, Cyber/AI Attacks, Civil War, and How Blockchain and a Survivorship Community Can Help, with Dr. Drew Miller @ Fortitude Ranch

Crypto Trading and Investing

- How to Best Empower Users to Manage Their Non-Custodial Wallets Intuitively, with Zhen Yu Yong @ Web3Auth

- How to Conduct Your Own Digital Asset Health Check and Ensure Your Crypto Investing Decisions are Sound, with Anthony Fernandez @ ICONOMI

- How to Avoid Getting Burned While Undertaking a Digital Security Revolution, with Michal "Mehow" Pospieszalski @ MatterFi

- Why Meme Coins Can Solve the Inherent Inequities of Financial Nihilism, with Rennick Palley @ Stratos

- Galileo FX CEO Shares His Insights On How Anyone Can Become An Expert Crypto Trader, with David Materazzi

- How to Uncover Hidden Stories Behind Crypto Prices and Use Custom Analytics to Solve Blind Spots in Your Investment Thesis, with Aakash Athawasya @ PYOR

- How to Avoid Chasing Greed and Illicit Activity During Crypto Bull Markets, with Phillip Alexeev @ CrossFi

- How to Become a Successful Crypto Trader by Developing a Winning Trading Mindset, with Casey Stubbs @ Global Prop Trader

- Optimizing the Crypto Trading Experience with Perpetual Futures for Bitcoin, Altcoins, and Meme Coins, with Mohd Kifa @ Flipster

- Helping Crypto Traders and Investors Take Advantage of the Best Strategic Opportunities to Generate Yield and Enhance Efficiency Through Liquid Staking, with Michael Wasyl @ Bracket

- Learn, Invest, Succeed—How Knowledge, Education, and Mindset Can Empower Investors and Traders to Navigate Crypto and Commodity Markets, with Mukarram Mawjood @ Bullionite Asset Group

- Crypto Hipster Presents...Shooting from the Hip! (Ep. 13): How to Spot Wash Trading, Rug Pulls, and Various Sordid Unethical Behaviors in Crypto Markets Easily; with Mathias Beke @ Kairon Labs

- Why Public Blockchain Wallets Are Dead and Privacy Matters Most, with Georgi Koreli @ Hinkal

- Making Digital Transactions Simple Through Text-to-Trade Functionality and "Hooting", with Dylan Dewdney @ Kuvi.ai

- Unlocking the Power of Decentralized Finance to Help Investors Stay Safe, Transact Ethically, and Gain Access to Web3, with James Toledano @ Savl

- Building a Secure, Robust, and Intelligent Web3 Wallet of the Future, with Alvin Kan @ Bitget Wallet

- Lessons and Insights from Helping Private Clients Invest in Crypto Successfully, with Marc Walton @ Forex Mentor Pro

- Whiskey, Wine, and Watches: Where Passion and Crypto Meet to Create New Investment Opportunities, with Sam Mudie @ Savea

- Crypto Hipster Presents...Shooting from the Hip! Episode 8: Safeguarding Investors Against Pump and Dump Schemes by Building a Best-in-Breed, Multiple Asset-Backed Cryptocurrency, with Jack McInerney

- The Challenges with Solving Inauthentic Web3 Washing, with Justin Banon @ Boson Protocol

- Building the World's First On-chain Order-book Exchange to Allow Users Full Control of Their Crypto Assets, with Vitali Dervoed @ Spark

- Transforming Family Offices and Innovating Special Purpose Vehicles for the Web3 Digital Age, with Jake Claver @ Digital Ascension Group

- How the UK is Helping Professional Crypto Investors by Enabling Exchange Traded Notes, with Oliver Linch @ Bittrex Global

- Options Trading, Digital Dollars, and Crypto Predictions for 2024, with Anthony Saliba @ Liquid Mercury

- Insights on the Future of Crypto Derivatives Trading, with Mark Lee @ SynFutures

- Why Crypto Options and Structured Products Can Help Manage Risk as We Head into the Bull Market, with Georgii Verbitskii @ TYMIO

- How to Transform Web3 Capital Allocations Through Successful Grant Funding Programs and Strategies, with Meg Lister @ Gitcoin Labs (Video)

- How to Leverage the Benefits of Automation Tools When Investing and Trading for the Next Decentralized Finance (DeFi) Summer, with Chris Bradbury @ Summer.Fi

- Preserving Security, Transparency, and Efficiency in Decentralized Trading Environments, with JOTARO @ JOJO

The Evolution of Decentralization

- Why Decentralization May Face an Existential Crisis During the Trump 2.0 Era and What We Can Do About It, with Josh Bowen @ Astria

- Crypto Hipster Presents… Shooting from the Hip! Episode 11: How the Crypto Industry is Successfully Recovering from the FTX Collapse, with Ishan Bhaidani @ SCRIB3

- Crypto Hipster Presents: Reporter on the Ground, Episode 1; Why Today's Tech Entrepreneurs Will Become Tomorrow's Successful Business Leaders, with Annelise Osborne @ Kadena

- How to Power the Borderless Global Economy and Bring Web Three to the World, with Raj Parekh @ Portal

- Crypto Hipster Presents: Shooting from the Hip!, Episode 3: Satoshi, Silk Road & Celsius: Building a Decentralized Over-Collateralized Stablecoin Protocol, with Joshua Scigala @ The Standard

- Envisioning a Web3 Bill of Rights for the Data Economy, with Jonathan Padilla @ Snickerdoodle Labs

- Building an Interconnected Network of Value to Bring Back Crypto's "Good Old Days" and Foster a Blockchain Renaissance, with Jerry Li @ Artela Network

- Crypto Hipster's Christmas Special: The Three Magi of Blockchain Technology: Speed, Security, and Scalability, with Dr. Alan Tominey @ Gorki

- How to Transform the Crypto Industry into a $100 Trillion Market Cap Opportunity, with Nick Cowan @ VLRM

- Crypto Hipster Presents: Reporter on the Ground, Episode 3; Why Zero-Knowledge is the Next Really Very Smart Trillion Dollar Opportunity, with Alex Pruden @ Aleo Network Foundation

- The Birth, Evolution, and Future of Zero Knowledge, with Kurt Hemecker @ Mina Foundation

- Building a Decentralized World of Knowledge Sharing and Data Verification, with Žiga Drev @ Trace Labs

- The Critical Importance of Building a Cloudless, Decentralized, Global Serverless Computing Network, with Tom Trowbridge @ Fluence Labs

- Leadership Insights from Building a Successful Full-Stack Blockchain Consulting Firm and Helping Clients Navigate the New Normal, with Vikram R Singh @ Antier Solutions

- How to Democratize Access to Money Issuance by Revolutionizing the Money Technology Stack, with Joao Reginatto @ M^ZERO Labs

- Why Multi-Signature Crypto Wallets Are Just a Band-Aid for a Much Larger Problem, with Simon McLoughlin @ Uphold

- $Y2 = X3 + 7$; Designing the Formula for the Future of Quantum-Resistant Computing, with Ian Smith @ Quantum EVM

- Crypto Hipster Presents...Shooting from the Hip! Ep 12: Why Designing Excellent Technological Standards Provides the Bedrock for Global Mass Adoption of Blockchain Technology; Fabian Vogelsteller @ LUKSO

- Quai, Qi, and the Serenity Effect of Transforming Compute Power into Money, with Alan Orwick @ Quai Network

- Building a Parallelized Confidential Computing Network that Helps Industries with Exposure to the Most Sensitive Data

Perform Encrypted Computations, with Yannik Schrade @ Arcium

- Discovering Why Social Experiences are the Best Way to Onboard the Next Hundred Million People into Web Three, with Chris Liquin @ Cupcake

- Manifesting and Rewarding Attestations by Creating Customizable Social Graphs to Filter Your Proprietary Data, with Billy Luedtke @ Intuition

- Solving the Sovereign Trilemma and Improving Liquidity in Modular Ecosystems, w/ Karel Kubat @ Union

- Bringing Together Fragmented Web3 Economies at the Southeast Asia Blockchain Week, with Nathan Kim @ UNOPND and Rachel Kim @ ShardLab

- Entering the Maitrix by Building an Economic Infrastructure for Decentralized AI, with Ian Estrada @ MAITRIX

- Why the Unsolvable Inefficiencies of Analog Traditional Financial Markets Open the Door for Digital Markets to Replace Them and Thrive in the Coming Years, with David Weisberger @ CoinRoutes

- A Hero's Journey: Reducing Fraud, Waste, and Theft and Transforming the Logistics Industry, with Todd Haselhorst @ HEALE Labs

- Why Smart Contracts and Data Capture Methods Must Continue to Evolve, with Nikhil Raghuveera @ Aethos

- The importance of capturing proof of authenticity while empowering a decentralized network of networks for the Web Three world, with Adam Helfgott @ Valence

Decentralized Finance (DeFi)

- The Future of Decentralized Finance is Here; It's Time for Regulators to Get on Board, with Hedi Navazan @ 1inch Group

- Why Consumer-Based DeFi Applications Are the Catalyst for Worldwide Blockchain Industry Adoption, with Cecilia Hsueh @ Morph

- Diving Into the "Down and Dirty" of Digging for Pristine DeFi Yield, with Nick Motz @ Soil

- How to Offer Decentralized Finance Yield-Earning Products in Emerging Market and High-Inflation Countries, with Max Galash @ Coinchange

- Redefining the Future of Decentralized Finance with Intents and Solvers, with Nikita Ovchinnik @ Barter DeFi

- Mixed Berries: Diving Into Decentralized Finance, Ethereum, NFTs, and More, with Jonathan Thomas @ Blueberry Protocol

- How to Build a DeFi Operating System that Drives Mainstream Adoption with Improved User Experiences, with James Lucas @ Lamina

- Discovering to Earn: Building Reward-Based Loyalty Programs; and the Importance of Recording Your Life's Achievements, with Jacob Margulies @ Galxe

- Building the Next Generation, Cross-Chain, Comprehensive Suite of Decentralized Finance Services, with Benedetto Biondi @ Folks Finance

- Pushing, Pulling, and Disentangling the Messy and Secretive World of Blockchain Oracles, with Chris Hermida @ Switchboard

- Crypto Hipster Presents: Reporter on the Ground, Episode 8; Exploring the Full Attestation of Blockchain Oracles, with Angus Tookey @ Chronicle

- Making DeFi Safer: How to Improve Cross-Chain Interoperability and Alleviate DeFi Vulnerabilities, with Mary McGilvray @ Interchain GmbH

- How to Develop a Single Ecosystem for Finance, Payments, and Trading Digital Assets, with Mike Romanenko @ Kyrrex

- How to Simplify Sophisticated DeFi Strategies for the Web3 World, with Kurapika @ Factor

- Exploring a Web3 OG Venture Capital Firm's Views on the Current Crypto Market and Decentralized Financial Landscape, with Alex Botte @ Hack VC

- Why Learning Chess Can Help You Rebalance Your Crypto Portfolio and Earn Greater Returns, with Danny Chong @ Tranchess

- Supercharging DeFi and Social AI Systems by Creating the Most Democratized Network, With Steven Pu @ Taraxa

- How Decentralized Networks Have Not Been Fully Decentralized and Why They Can Be Now, with Victor Vernissage @ Humanode.io

- Envisioning the Future of Decentralized Oracles and the Best Way to Help Traditional Financial Organizations Adopt Web3, with Marc Tillement @ Pyth Network

- Crypto Hipster Presents: Shooting from the Hip!, Episode 6: Why Smart Contracts Are Not Quite Smart Enough for the Mainstream DeFi User., with Adam Simmons @ RDX Works

- How to Help Startups and Institutions Empower Global Finance for the New Millenium, with Evan Owens @ Kadena

- How Restaking is Empowering an Open, Trustworthy Market and Why Crypto Regulators Should Take a 1990s Bill Clinton Internet Approach, with Warren Anderson @ Exocore

- How Syrup Can Achieve Stickiness in the Global Institutional DeFi Market, with Martin de Rijke @ Syrup, powered by Maple Finance

- How to Develop and Promote Blockchain Loyalty Reward Infrastructures, with Gabriele Giancola @ qiibee Foundation

- Designing Blockchain-Based Insurance Solutions to Mitigate Crypto Risks and Move Web3 Forward Powerfully, with Joseph Ziolkowski @ Relm Insurance

- Creating the First and Largest Liquid Staking and Re-staking Protocol in the Modular Ecosystem, with Josie Leung @ MilkyWay

- Building the First-of-Its-Kind, Permissionless DeFi Clearinghouse, with Barna Kiss @ Malda

- How the Web3 sector can combat the pertinent and costly issue of Maximal Extractable Value (MEV), with Da Hongfei, founder of Neo

- Overcoming the Challenges Facing Automated Market Makers and How to Avoid Unnecessary DeFi Costs, with Sunil Srivatsa @ Storm Labs

- Offering Sophisticated, Seamless, and Secure Innovations to Help Deliver Web3 Banking Solutions of the Future, with Myles Harrison @ AMINA Bank

Blockchain Education

- Why Raising the Benchmark in Blockchain Education is Important, with Cy Li @ Ethereum Collective Foundation

- Democratizing Blockchain Education as a First Step to Solving Web3 Developer Shortages, with David Bchiri @ XRPL Commons

Ethereum

- Leading the Charge to Safeguard and Enhance Ethereum's Historical Data Availability, with Ganesh Swami @ Covalent

- A Call to Action to Save Ethereum From Impending Disaster, with Alon Muroch @ SSV Labs

- Uncovering The Secret to Saving Ethereum Users Billions of Dollars in Transaction Fees, with Spring Dunn @ SKALE Labs

Fantasy Sports, Betting, and Entertainment

- Exploring the Future of Decentralized Sports Betting with Data-Driven Intelligence and Smart Leverage, with Mr. Blue @ LEVR.bet

- Why Karate Combat Is Appealing to the Younger Generations and How Fans and Influencers Can Drive the Future of Game Streaming Forward, with Kyle "Post Master" @ Karate Combat

- Re-imagining Sports Book Betting by Enabling Users to Be the House, with Peter Argerakis @ Six Sigma Sports

- Helping Brands Take Control of Their Narratives Through Fandom-Driven Experiences, with Anthony Rodriguez @ The Digital Spenders Club

- Creating the First Web3 Fantasy League for Movie Fans, with Stacy Spikes @ Mogul by MoviePass

- Creating an Online Casino at the Crossroads of Crypto and Culture, with Zach Bruch @ MyPrize

- Shark, Pickle, Cone Documentary Movie to Debut on May 29th at Consensus 2024, with

Chris Waters and Neil Berkeley @ Stoopid
Buddy Stoodios

Web3 Gaming

- Challenging the Public Perception of What Web3 Gaming Should Be, with Max Fu @ Nyan Heroes

- The Challenges and Experiences Behind Building the World's Largest Social and Casual Web3 Game, with Luke Barwikowski @ Pixels

- Crypto Hipster Presents: Reporter on the Ground, Episode 2; How to Help Gaming Studios Stop Flying Blind, with Lucas Fulks @ Helika

- Still Focusing on the Fun: Helping Developers, Content Creators, and Game Players Build the Future of Web Three Gaming, with Marc Mercuri @ Shrapnel

- How to Transform the Gaming and Advertising Industries With Decentralized Payment Solutions, with Timothy Tello @ 3thix

- Creating a World Development Gaming Studio at the Intersection of Blockchain and AI, with Ilman Shazhaev @ Dizzaract
- Creating a Fun Ultimate Playground for Gamers to Unlock Web3 Experiences, with Daniel Anthony @ ZKcandy

- Transforming Normies into Degens with Progressive Web App Games, with Tomer Pascal @ OwnPlay

- Slaying the Bear and Building the Future of Sustainable Web3 Strategy Gaming, with David Johansson @ BLOCKLORDS

Identity, Storage, and Commerce

- How to Drive Innovative Breakthroughs in the Decentralized Digital Identity Space, with Harrison Seletsky @ SPACE ID

- Examining the Current Decentralized Storage Landscape to Help AI Fulfill Its Potential in Web3, with Ryan Levy @ DataHaven / Moonbeam

- Discovering the Parallels Between Blockchain Advancements and the Evolution of Multi-Channel E-Commerce, with Neil Twa @ Voltage Holdings

- Combatting AI-Driven Fraud Using Crypto File Storage Solutions, with Kyle Tut @ Pinata

Intellectual Property / Thought Leadership

- How to Discover Market-Redefining Opportunities and Support Emerging Entrepreneurs in Web3 and Beyond, with Jameel Qeblawi @ myqubator

- All Aboard the Ideas Sled!: Leveraging Innovative Technology to Inspire and Influence Change with Grace, with Christopher G. Fox, PhD @ Ideas-Led Growth

- Crypto Hipster Presents: Reporter on the Ground, Episode 6; Discovering How a Cookie Can Disrupt the Global Digital Marketing Industry without Crumbling, with Krystyna Kozak-Kornacka @ Cookie3

- How to Create Your Self-Sovereign Social Identity with Proof of Humanity, with Lasha Antadze @ Rarify Labs (Part 2 of 2)

- How to Build a Brand People Can Trust in Nascent Industries, with Armel Leslie @ RF|Binder

- How to Position Your Web3 Brand at the Forefront of the Real-World Asset (RWA) Movement, with Bhaji Illuminati @ Centrifuge

- Telling Stories, Building Trust, and Helping Web3 Brands Succeed, with Samantha Yap @ YAP Global

- Discovering a World-Building, Immersive Platform for Creators by Creators, with Justin Melillo @ MONA

- Designing a Revolutionary Platform to Transform How Intellectual Property Ownership Is Created, Shared, and Monetized on Web3, with Jaime Schwarz @ MRKD

- Helping Web3 Micro-Influencers and Small Creative Agencies Gain Massive Audiences, with Ryan Davis @ People First
- Realizing the Benefits of Treating Your Web3 Community as CEO, with Kelsey McGuire @ Shardeum

- Building an Avant-Garde Social Gaming Platform that Empowers the New Creator Economy, with Casey Grooms @ Soulbound

Litecoin

- **Embracing a** Brighter Vision for the Future of Litecoin **and** Its Global Adoption in 2025 **and Beyond,** with David Schwartz @ Litecoin Foundation

Macroeconomic Outlook

- Why the Macroeconomic Outlook for Crypto in the U.S. is Extremely Bullish Despite Recent Short-Term Market Volatility, with Kyle Reidhead @ Milk Road

- Crypto Hipster Presents...Shooting from the Hip! Episode TEN. Insights from Argentina: Marrying Traditional Finance's Stability with Blockchain's Innovation Potential, with Agustin Liserra @ Num

- Crypto Hipster Presents...Shooting from the Hip! (E15): Why 2024 Will Be the Year that Crypto-Focused Voters Tip the U.S. Election Results in Pro-Blockchain Candidates' Favor, with Matthew Le Merle

- Crypto Payment Insights and Predictions for the Upcoming Bull Market, with Sean Mackay @ CoinPayments

- How SHOPX is Empowering Customer Ownership in Web 3, and How to Navigate this Current Inflationary Period Successfully, with TJ Chang @ SHOPX.

Mobility

- How to Revolutionize the Ride-Sharing Economy Through Web3 Innovation, with Firdosh Sheikh @ DRIFE

- Crypto Hipster Presents...Shooting from the Hip! (Ep 9): Shaping the Decentralized Future of Mobility Markets, with Deniz and Marko @ Soarchain

Non-Fungible Tokens (NFTs)

- Why NFTs May Still Just Be the Catalyst That Brings Billions of Web2 Users into Web3, with Aka Leung @ Bitget

- Season 7 Premiere: Solving Experiential and Developer Challenges with Web Three Gaming, Digital Collectibles, and NFTs, with Dr. Alun Evans @ LAOS Network

- Solving the Greatest Challenges Facing the Cannabis Industry with NFTs, with Ricardo Capone @ Dr. Green NFT

- Breaking Down Ivory Towers and Stone Walls: How NFTs Can Enhance Life Experiences and Benefit Local Communities, with Tyler Adams @ COZ

- Alive and Kickin': Why NFTs Are Far From Dead; Rather, an NFT-Future Looks Quite Bright, with Rusty Matveev @ Calaxy

- Revolutionizing the Best of Both Traditional Art and Digital Art Worlds with Digital Twin NFTs [SEASON 6 FINALE], with Zain Talyarkhan @ Notable.art

Regulatory and Compliance

- How to Blend Fiat and Crypto Payments in a Secure and Compliant Way, with Nikolay Denisenko @ Brighty

- How to Navigate the Global Crypto Regulatory Environment Successfully, with Norman Wooding @ SCRYPT

- Cutting through the Bullsh*t U.S. Regulatory Hurdles to Help Provide Your Institution's CFO Office with Crypto Financial Reporting Solutions that Genuinely Work, w/ Amy Kalnoki and Pat White @ Bitwave

- Why KYC, AML, and Black Swan Insurance are Essential Pillars to Onboard Institutions into Decentralized Protocols, with Ramon Recuero @ Kinto

- Helping Virtual Asset Service Providers Navigate the New Travel Rule Requirements Globally, with Emeka Mgbenu @ Sumsub

- Why Using the Telegram Platform for Compliant Digital Asset Trading is the New Frontier, with Chilip Lai @ LeapXpert

- Helping Enterprises Navigate MiCA by Providing a Comprehensive Solution for

Managing Digital Assets, with Tom Kiddle @ Palisade

- Tackling the Complexities of Legally Compliant Fungibility for Stablecoin Issuers in Europe Under MiCA Regulations, with Gijs Op De Weegh @ StablR

Real-World Asset (RWA) Tokenization

- Overcoming the Challenges of Tokenizing and Fractionalizing Real-World Assets, with Graeme Moore @ Polymesh Association

- Why the Tokenization of Real-World Assets Will Front-Run Traditional Finance, with Niklas Kunkel @ Chronicle Labs

- How to Bring Real-World Tokenized Assets (RWAs) to the Masses, with Chris Yin @ Plume

- Tokenizing the World: Why the Future of Crypto and Blockchain Technology is the Mass Tokenization of Real-World Assets, with Carlos Balbin

- Designing the First Genuinely Global Tokenized Infrastructure and Decentralized Real World Asset (RWA) Marketplace, with Miguel Buffara @ RACE

- The Importance of Creating a Multi-Chain Asset Tokenization Launchpad that Tokenizes Any Asset, with Jeroen Offerijns @ Centrifuge

- Crypto Hipster Presents: Shooting from the Hip!, Episode 4: The Impending Rapture for Tokenizing Real-World Assets and the Resurrection of Satoshi Nakamoto's Original Bitcoin Vision, with Jonny Fry

- Real World Assets, Democratizing Access to Data, and the Advantages of Decentralization, with Stefan Rust @ Truflation

- Bringing Real-World Assets (RWAs) On-Chain for Low-Cost Financing and Regenerating the NFT Market, Kkrusher (Kevin Rusher) @ RAAC

- Unlocking Tokenized Ownership in the World's Most Luxurious Resorts, with Ricardo Johnson @ Oases

- How to Leverage Blockchain Technology to Secure Smooth, Efficient, and Trustworthy Real Estate Transactions, with Erik LaPaglia @ Propy

- Using the Internet of Things, Machine Learning and Blockchain Technology to Help Farmers in Marginalized Areas, with Jon Trask @ Dimitra

- Tokenizing GPUs and Their Yields to Create a New Asset Class for AI and Compute, with Kony @ GAIB

- How to Transform Access to Compute by Creating GPU Financial Assets, with Nikolay Filichkin @ Compute Labs

- How to Transform Idle Tokens Into Productive Assets, with Altan Tutar @ MoreMarkets

- Transforming Real-World Compute Into On-Chain Assets Through Mining Hardware Tokenization, with Leo Fan Xiong @ Cysic

Social Impact

- Discovering a New Currency, a New Financial Freedom, and a New World, with Dr. Karl Huber @ Quai Network

- Decentralization: The Bridge to Abundance for Humanity, with Violet Abtahi @ Platonic

- Girl Talk, Taking Risks, and Creating Timeless Classics in a Blockchain World, with Claire Ross-Brown @ CJ London

- "I Have a Dream!": Building a Valuable Global Economy and Collaborative World Society Together, with Web3 Technology, Ethos, and Values, with Anjali Young @ Collab.Land

- Reforming Socio-Economic Systems to Facilitate the Generation and Spread of Natural Wealth via Energy, Finance, and Bitcoin Mining, with Mohamed El-Masri @ Hodler

- Exploring Humanity's Role in a Super-Intelligence AI-Driven Future, with Jamie Goldblatt @ Mind Chill AI—Cyberverse of Chill

- 4th of July 2024 Special: How to Chart Your Personal Independence Into the Web Three World through AI and Blockchain Technology, with J.D. Seraphine @ Raiinmaker

- Recognizing and Celebrating Innovative Technologies That Can Improve Our Daily Lives and Ensure America Will Thrive in the Modern Digital Arena, with Joy Schoffler @ Distinctive Edge Partners

- Crypto Hipster Presents: Shooting from the Hip, Episode 2: Promoting Sustainable Development and Economic Empowerment in Ghana, with Ibrahim Mustapha @ Me for Africa

- Crypto Hipster Presents: Shooting from the Hip! (E5): How a Tech Maverick with an Unwavering Commitment to Preserving People's Rights to Privacy is Reshaping the Global Digital World, with JB Benjamin

- Solving the Current Challenges with Using Crypto as a Payment Method for the World's Spanish-Speaking Population, with Javier Castro-Acuña @ Bitnovo

- Empowering Users and Marginalized Communities by Sharing Hotspot

Connections and Enabling Access to Web Three, with Ugochukwu Aronu @ Wicrypt

- Helping Retail Consumers Thrive by Transforming Web3 Ecosystems to Adopting an Inclusive Economic Model Instead of a Player-versus-Player Trap, with Cyrus Taghehchian @ Aces.Fun

- Crypto Hipster Presents: Reporter on the Ground, Episode 7; Creating Collaborative Innovation through Social Capitalism, with John Wingate @ Bank Social

- Crypto Hipster Presents: Reporter on the Ground, Episode 9; Creating a New Unified Experiential Society, with John Vibes @ Somnia

- Charting New Paths for Humanity to Preserve the Potential of People Amidst an Ever-Increasing Artificial Intelligence Revolution, with Terence Kwok @ Humanity Protocol

Solana

- How to Design the Most Flexible and Efficient Staking Strategies and Experiences for Solana Users, with Michael Repetny @ Marinade

- Insights From Building Solana's First Meta Decentralized Exchange Aggregator, with Chris Chung @ Titan

- Why Ethereum Must Be Saved Soon, and How the Solana Virtual Machine Can Help, with Joanna Zeng @ SOON

- Advancements in Oracles and the Evolution of Solana Beyond Simply "Sam's Coin", with Mitchell Gildenberg @ Switchboard

Sustainability

- Leveraging Distributed Ledger Technology to Create ESG Impact Initiatives that Facilitate Sustainability, Reliability and Integrity, with Andrew Forson @ The Hashgraph Association

- Solving Greenwashing, Environmental Propaganda, and the United Nations' Biodiversity Challenges with Generational Blockchain Technology, with Owen O'Driscoll @ Trrue

- How to Build a Decentralized Movement for Emissions Reporting to Ensure Accurate Business Sustainability Claims, with Caitlin Moore @ Filecoin Green

- How the Intersection of AI, ESG Investing, and Carbon Credit Tokenization Can Help the United Nations Meet Their Sustainability Goals, with Daniel Steeves

The Digital Economist

- How to Leverage Blockchain and Sustainable Innovative Technology to Drive Economic, Environmental, and Social Advancements Globally, with Dr. Nikhil Varma

- How Socioeconomic Forces Driving an AI Revolution Will Lead to Advancements in Human Evolution, with Dr. Shruti Shankar Gaur @ The Digital Economist

- Guest Episode 500: Innovation, Inspiration, and the Rise of the Tech-Infused Entrepreneur, with Jean Criss @ The Digital Economist; Jean Criss Media; CRISSCROSS Intimates

- How to Nationalize Digital Currencies, With Lessons From Implementing Chivo Bitcoin Wallet in El Salvador, with Tristan Thoma @ Impera Strategy

Appendix D: Crypto Hipster's Mysticals Books on Amazon.com

These books are the Crypto Hipster Mysticals episodes from Seasons Four and Five, as published in book format on Amazon. They are compilations of three or more episodes captured primarily for readers and historians. There are twenty-two books in the Crypto Hipster's Mysticals compilation, with another seventy-three plus books under various collections.

- The Sword of Ja-million: The Future of Web Three Gaming in a Globally Decentralized World (Crypto Hipster's Mysticals Book 1)
- Savory Wild RICE: Rights, Inspiration, Currency, and Enthusiasm for the People with Blockchain Technology (Crypto Hipster's Mysticals Book 2)
- Unreal, Surreal, or Artificially Real?: Influencing the World Through a Rapidly Growing Artificial Intelligence and

Blockchain Technology Landscape (Crypto Hipster's Mysticals Book 3)

- Sugary Maple Eggs and Scrambled Bacon: The Future of Crypto Platforms, Infrastructure, and Decentralized Autonomous Organizations (Crypto Hipster's Mysticals Book 4)
- Hot Steamy Luggage: How Artificial Intelligence, Blockchain, and the Metaverse Can Restore Humanity (Crypto Hipster's Mysticals Book 5)
- Hot Spicy Luggage: Regulatory Affairs, Attacks on Privacy, and Why Governments Need Central Bank Digital Currencies (Crypto Hipster's Mysticals Book 6)
- Hot Smoky Luggage: A Spot Check Inventory on Crypto Market Prices From 2023 (Crypto Hipster's Mysticals Book 7)
- Hot Sapid Luggage: Ushering in a Prosperous Decentralized Finance Future (Crypto Hipster's Mysticals Book 8)
- Hot Scrumptious Luggage: Sustainability and Dominion: Bridging the Divide Between the Abstract and the Concrete (Crypto Hipster's Mysticals Book 9)
- Not Just All About Cats, Dogs, Sloths, and Other Fuzzy Digital Creatures, Volume One: The Staggering Distance Between a JPEG and a Carbon Copy of Reality (Crypto Hipster's Mysticals Book 10)
- Not Just All About Cats, Dogs, Sloths, and Other Fuzzy Digital Creatures, Volume Two:

Pushing Through Web2 Barriers to Share Your Voice on Web3 (Crypto Hipster's Mysticals Book 11)

- Not Just All About Cats, Dogs, Sloths, and Other Fuzzy Digital Creatures, Volume Three: Transforming Finance's Future and Building Unbreakable Infrastructure (Crypto Hipster's Mysticals Book 12)
- Overcoming Crypto Catastrophes: Helping the World Embrace the Transition from Web2 to Web3 (Crypto Hipster's Mysticals Book 13)
- You Can Hear It Through the Block-Vine: Master Your Fear, Uncertainty and Doubt with Crypto as the Anchor of Trust (Crypto Hipster's Mysticals Book 14)
- Bright Vibrant Skies or Blurry Muddy Puddles?: Staring into the Abyss of an Orwellian Dystopia...or the Abundance of a Vivid Bitcoin Utopia (Crypto Hipster's Mysticals Book 15)
- Furry Psychedelic Crypto Tokens: Why Social Justice, Diversity, and Inclusion in Web3 Are Far More Than Just Feel-Good Hype Phrases (Crypto Hipster's Mysticals Book 16)
- Blame It On The Blockchain: Milli Jamilli Redux: Why Blockchain Data Is Much More Than Just Data Recorded on a Blockchain! (Crypto Hipster's Mysticals Book 17)
- Crypto Journeys Are Burning Like Wildfire: How Founders and Developers Are Creating

Opportunities for Self-Sovereign Web3 Journeys (Crypto Hipster's Mysticals Book 18)

- Let's Play Checkers; Let's Play Risk...Yes, Yeh, Yea, Yeah!!: Overcoming Challenges Facing Communities in Decentralized Social Finance, Gaming, and Web3 Media (Crypto Hipster's Mysticals Book 19)
- Choosing Peace in a Turbulent World: How Cryptocurrencies Can Serve As a Safe Haven During Challenging Political Times (Crypto Hipster's Mysticals Book 20)
- A Father's Cry For Help: How a Courageous Father Persevered Against an International Criminal Conspiracy to Seek Justice for His Son (Crypto Hipster's Mysticals Book 21)
- Everyday People: The Web3 Version: Our Global, Social, Financial, and Economic Future is Decentralized (Crypto Hipster's Mysticals Book 22)

Appendix E: Crypto Hipster's Chronicles Books on Amazon.com

These books are the Crypto Hipster Chronicles episodes from Seasons One, Two, and Three, as published in book format on Amazon. They are compilations of three or more episodes captured primarily for readers and historians. There are forty-six books in the Crypto Hipster's Chronicles compilation, with another two-hundred plus books under various collections.

- Old Paradigms Die Hard: Proof of Resilience: How Ukraine Built a Sovereign Digital Economy in the Face of War with Russia (Crypto Hipster's Chronicles Book 1)

- From Stuck to Unstoppable: How Blockchain Technology Can Help You Overcome Adversity, Depression, and Suicidal

Thoughts (Crypto Hipster's Chronicles Book 2)

- Why Wall Street Is Running Scared: How Decentralized Finance Has the Titans of Wall Street Shaking in Their Suits (Crypto Hipster's Chronicles Book 3)

- Origins of the Metaverse: How the Metaverse is Metamorphosizing the Future of Digital Technology (Crypto Hipster's Chronicles Book 4)

- An Altruistic New Paradigm: The Pursuit of Trust and Altruistic Good (Crypto Hipster's Chronicles Book 5)

- A State in a Smartphone: A Safe Harbor for Ukraine (Crypto Hipster's Chronicles Book 6)

- Play Amazing Games, Earn Amazing Prizes: The Play-to-Earn Benefits of Crypto Gaming (with Ancients and Heroes) (Crypto Hipster's Chronicles Book 7)

- The Zoology and Cheese of NFTs: The Many Shapes and Sizes of Non-Fungible Tokens (NFTs)... For You's and For Me's (Crypto Hipster's Chronicles Book 8)

- The Crypto Nomad's Powerful Brew: How Decentralization Combats Frauds, Rugs, and Digital Crime (Crypto Hipster's Chronicles Book 9)

- Sold Out in Fifteen Seconds: NFTs for Gaming, Art, Investments, Graffiti, and Digital Disneyland (Crypto Hipster's Chronicles Book 10)

- Knowledge is Power: How The Knowledge Society Helps Students Make a Significant Impact in the World (Crypto Hipster's Chronicles Book 11)

- Trees, Birds, and Fire: How Musicians and Artists Can Leverage Web 3.0 to Build Fan Engagement (Crypto Hipster's Chronicles Book 12)

- Cats and Cancer, Iron and Power: How NFT Artists and Entrepreneurs are Overcoming Adversity and Building Resiliency with Blockchain Technology (Crypto Hipster's Chronicles Book 13)

- The Crypto Nomad's Galactic Journey: Scooters, EVs, and Outer Space with Blockchain, Sustainability, and Hustle, Baby!! (Crypto Hipster's Chronicles Book 14)

- Metaverse Challenges Beneath Z Hype: Exploring Research, Development, and Logistics of Crypto Gaming and the Metaverse (Crypto Hipster's Chronicles Book 15)

- My Web3 NFT Went to the Market: Early Web3 and NFT Marketplaces and Healthcare

Benefits While Not Staying Home (Crypto Hipster's Chronicles Book 16)

- Fierce... Courageous... Heroes: Creating a World of Heroes with Bitcoin and NFTs (Crypto Hipster's Chronicles Book 17)

- Mitigating Crypto Control Risks: Addressing Crypto Compliance and Global Regulatory Standards (Crypto Hipster's Chronicles Book 18)

- The Digital Path For Global Sustainability Goals: Achieving Global Sustainability Goals through Bitcoin Mining and Community Coins (Crypto Hipster's Chronicles Book 19)

- Valley and Thunder; Springtime and Crypto Winter: Early Predictions and Trends from 2022 (Crypto Hipster's Chronicles Book 20)

- Privacy, Data Ownership, and Freedom in the Web Three Era: Controlling and Securing Your Personal Web 3 Data and Online Identity (Crypto Hipster's Chronicles Book 21)

- Breaking: Wall Street; Why: Bitcoin: Why Bitcoin is Impervious to Overreaching Bureaucrats and Unethical Politicians (Crypto Hipster's Chronicles Book 22)

- Cash Flows in Crypto Valley: How Switzerland is Poised to Become the Global

Crypto Leader (Crypto Hipster's Chronicles
Book 23)

- Governance, Intelligence, and Justice: Three
Pillars of Decentralized Autonomous
Organizations (Crypto Hipster's Chronicles
Book 24)

- Solving the Carbon Neutrality Crisis:
Discovering Bitcoin Mining's Beneficial
Impact for the Environment (Crypto
Hipster's Chronicles Book 25)

- Bitcoin Ethics in a Corrupted World: Are We
Achieving Satoshi Nakamoto's Vision or
Simply Succumbing to Unethical
"Regulators"? (Crypto Hipster's Chronicles
Book 26)

- Persevering Greatly in an Ocean of
Unqualified Critics: Building a Resiliency
Skill Set through Recreating Memories,
Empowering Women, and Fighting for ...
World (Crypto Hipster's Chronicles Book 27)

- War... and Peace... and... Altruism: War
Games, Utility Tokens, AK47s, and
Blockchain for Peace (Crypto Hipster's
Chronicles Book 28)

- The Futurrr(e-2r) of Finance: DeFi-N-ing the
Future of Finance for Widespread Crypto
Adoption (Crypto Hipster's Chronicles Book
29)

- Stompin'!... by a Tree Trunk on a Snowy Evening: Uplifting Creators and NFT Collectors through Cutting-Edge Technologies and Zero-Knowledge Innovation (Crypto Hipster's Chronicles Book 30)

- Crypto: The Empire of the Shun?: Ethics, Conviction, and Resiliency—Important Personal Traits or Blockchain Cornerstones? (Crypto Hipster's Chronicles Book 31)

- Oogie! Groovy!! Boogie!!! DeFi Inferno!!!!: Funds, Crypto Banks, and Alternative Investments: Doing Decentralized Finance (DeFi) in Different Ways (Crypto Hipster's Chronicles Book 32)

- Burn Rubber and Chill Your Mind: Creating Equitable Futures and Healthy Ecosystems with Crypto Tokens, NFTs, and Metaverses (Crypto Hipster's Chronicles Book 33)

- Human Nature: Hipsters, Heroes, and Handbooks: Discover Your Inner NFT in the Real World and in the Metaverse (Crypto Hipster's Chronicles Book 34)

- Crypto Hipster: Crypto Hipster's 100th Episode: Untold Insights with Bitcoin Legend Charlie Shrem (Crypto Hipster's Chronicles Book 35)

- Sweeter Than a Reggie Bar: A Critical Look for Us Beyond Just Web Three (Crypto Hipster's Chronicles Book 36)

- The Superfreaky Groove Is in Your Heart: Starting from Zero and Building a Powerful Personal Blueprint for Success (Crypto Hipster's Chronicles Book 37)

- Boys to Chads: Motown Cryptodelphia: How the Blockchain Helps Content Creators Build Bright and Abundant Futures (Crypto Hipster's Chronicles Book 38)

- 100X Marks the "Oh, Gee!" Spot: Pitfalls and Rewards of Crypto Trading and Investing (Crypto Hipster's Chronicles Book 39)

- Sashay, Shante, & Prêt-À-Porter: (Ransomware, Gem Wear, and Underwear): Measuring Blockchain's Beneficial Impact on Disparate Industries (Crypto Hipster's Chronicles Book 40)

- The Rejuvenating Power of Sweet, Sweet Doctor Love: Empowering Healthcare Participants and Real Estate Owners in the Web 3 Economy (Crypto Hipster's Chronicles Book 41)

- Purply Fire, Orangey Rain, and the Funky Green Sandstorm of Freedom: Crypto Across Four Corners: Blockchain Insights from Around the World (Crypto Hipster's Chronicles Book 42)

- Securities, Tunnels, and the Surprisingly Delightful Splendor of Entropy: Creating a Path Forward in Decentralized Finance for Global Banks and Institutions (Crypto Hipster's Chronicles Book 43)

- The Unequivocal Usurpingly Manifesting Powerful Strength of the Spec..., Spec..., Spectacularly Spectacular Triangle Mindset (Crypto Hipster's Chronicles Book 44)

- Golden Fire in Your New Bitcoin Shoes: Why Economists and Environmentalists Are Often Wrong About Bitcoin (Crypto Hipster's Chronicles Book 45)

- Block Berry, Block Banana, and Block Sky Action: The Digital Crypto Future is Coming Sooner Than You Think (Crypto Hipster's Chronicles Book 46)

Appendix F: Full Season Crypto Hipster Compilations and Other Notable Books by the Author

Crypto Hipster's Full Season Compilations

Crypto Hipster: Crypto Hipster Podcast: The Complete First Season (March 1, 2021—June 30, 2021) (Crypto Hipster's Full Season Compilations)

Crypto Hipster: Crypto Hipster Podcast: The Complete Second Season (August 1, 2021—December 31, 2021) (Crypto Hipster's Full Season Compilations)

Crypto Hipster: Crypto Hipster Podcast: The Complete Third Season (January 1, 2022—June 30, 2022) (Crypto Hipster's Full Season Compilations)

Crypto Hipster: Crypto Hipster Podcast: The Complete Fourth Season (August 31, 2022—December 31, 2022)

Crypto Hipster's Golden Splendor: Crypto Hipster Podcast: The Complete Fifth Season (January 1, 2023—August 19, 2023)

Blockchain Ethics

Blockchain Ethics: A Bridge to Abundance

Blockchain Ethics: Arise from the Ashes

Blockchain Ethics: Fighting Honorable Battles

Generation X Manifesto

Re-Generation X: How Generation X Can Leverage Blockchain Technology to Save Themselves and Rebuild America

Appendix G: Author Jamil Hasan in the Media

Jamil Hasan - Crypto Planet (11/8/2017)

https://www.youtube.com/watch?v=eWiI52yTyes

Jamil Hasan Live from Studio 6B (3/28/2018)

https://www.youtube.com/watch?v=y3cTVoedFsc

Jamil Hasan Daily Magic Interview (7/12/2018)

https://www.youtube.com/watch?v=1fHrT8dIg5g

Jamil Hasan Spotlight TV Interview (7/28/2018)

https://www.youtube.com/watch?v=OubIQ5G6gqw

Naked Marketing #028 - Jamil Hasan - Marketing Mistake - Switching strategies too often (9/22/2021)

https://www.youtube.com/watch?v=_U_T3D5Izc
M

**METAVERSE INTERVIEWS with LeDrop
WithCheese - Episode 4 w/guest Jamil
Hasan, blockchain author and thought
leader** (7/28/2022)

https://www.youtube.com/watch?app=desktop&v=
qwss7YxXzug

**The Crypto Corner podcast with Jamil
Hasan: Moving Hemp Forward** (8/17/2022)

https://www.youtube.com/watch?v=FEgmftGQ19I

**Conversation with the Publisher of Crypto
Hipster Publications, Jamil Hasan, on the
Influencers Podcast with Dr. Bill Williams**
(1/23/2023)

https://www.youtube.com/watch?v=3D8Z7IUovco

**S2E2 Crypto With English with Jamil Hasan,
DeFi Author & Host of the "Crypto Hipster"**
(6/9/2023)

https://www.youtube.com/watch?app=desktop&v=
Nfsokpkc_e4

ThriveMore with Roger Martin: E138: Jamil Hasan: Crypto Investing 101: Making Sense of Blockchain and Bitcoin (7/2/2025)

https://www.youtube.com/watch?v=V2Q5V8PSSxQ

www.ingramcontent.com/pod-product-compliance
Lightning Source LLC
Chambersburg PA
CBHW030920060726

47591CB00005B/1617

9 781972 991008